Brilliant Dogs

Coloring Book for Adults

50 Different Dogs

Be an artist yourself

Produced by

INTELLIGENT
PRESS

what
zavion
poop
Big
changes

Book & Cover Design by **Intelligent Press LLC**
www.facebook.com/IntelligentPress
ISBN-10: 1979447322
ISBN-13: 978-1979447324

Preface

The art of coloring has a long history. Coloring patterns can be found in many ancient cultures, from the Greeks, to the Egyptians and even the Mayans. They all used beautiful patterns in their artwork. Today, people all over the world take advantage of coloring stress therapy for enjoyable relaxation.

This coloring book was created to be perfect for dog lovers. Combining the twin concepts of coloring stress relief and lovely dogs, we created **50** different dog coloring pages for you to paint.

Every page of this book allows you to express yourself; you open your soul by filling every single element on the picture with different colors. So, make your favorite drink, grab a few pencils; and now just sit and enjoy the book specially made just for you.

Thank you for purchasing this book.

Intelligent Press LLC

Try Your Colors Here

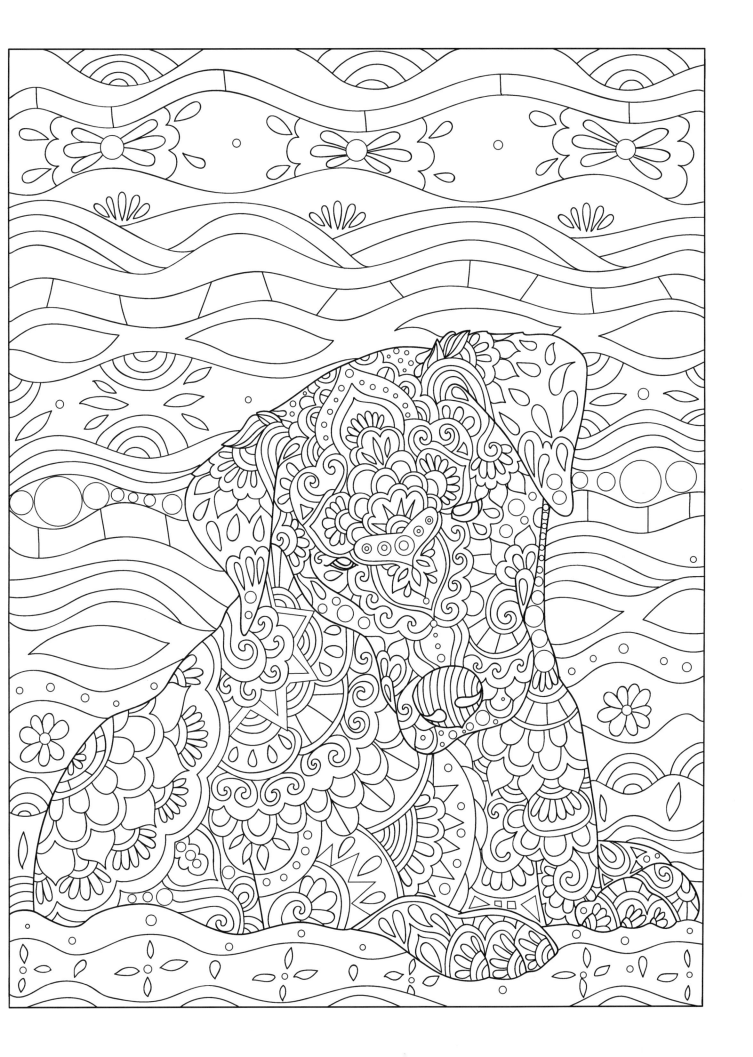

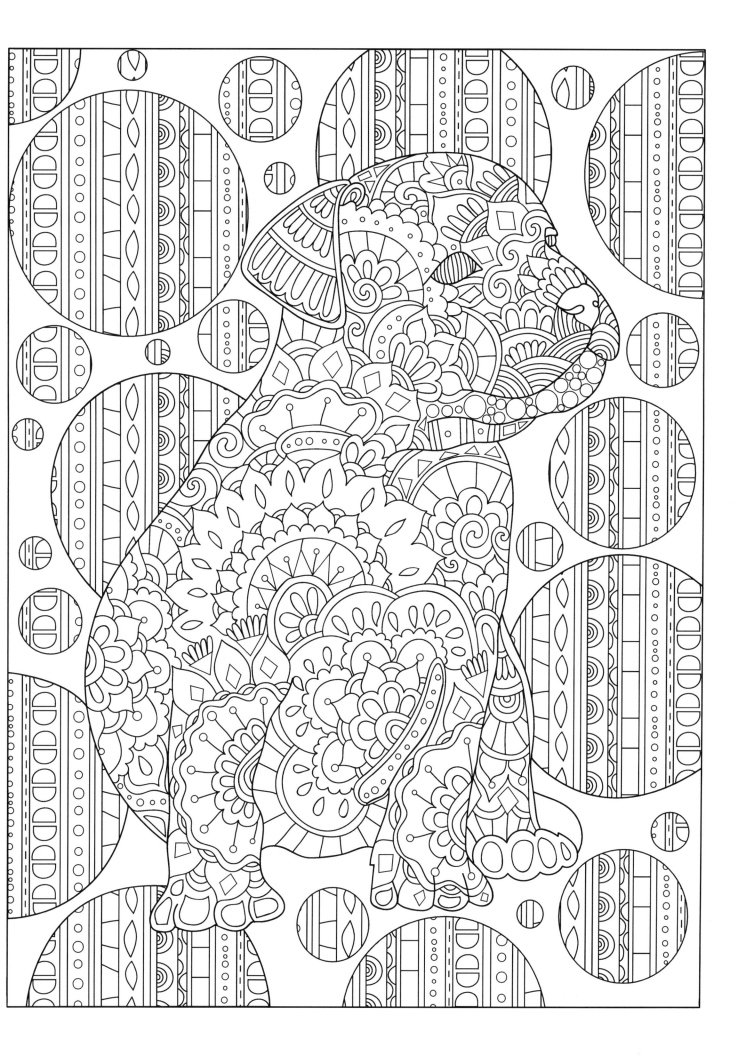

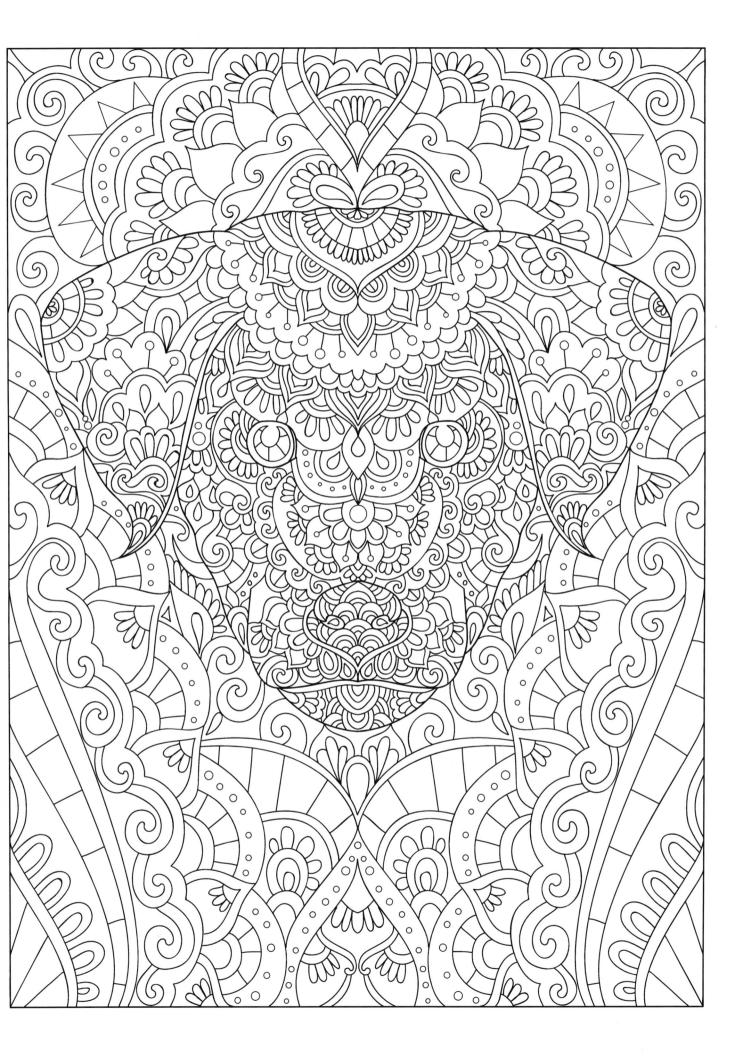

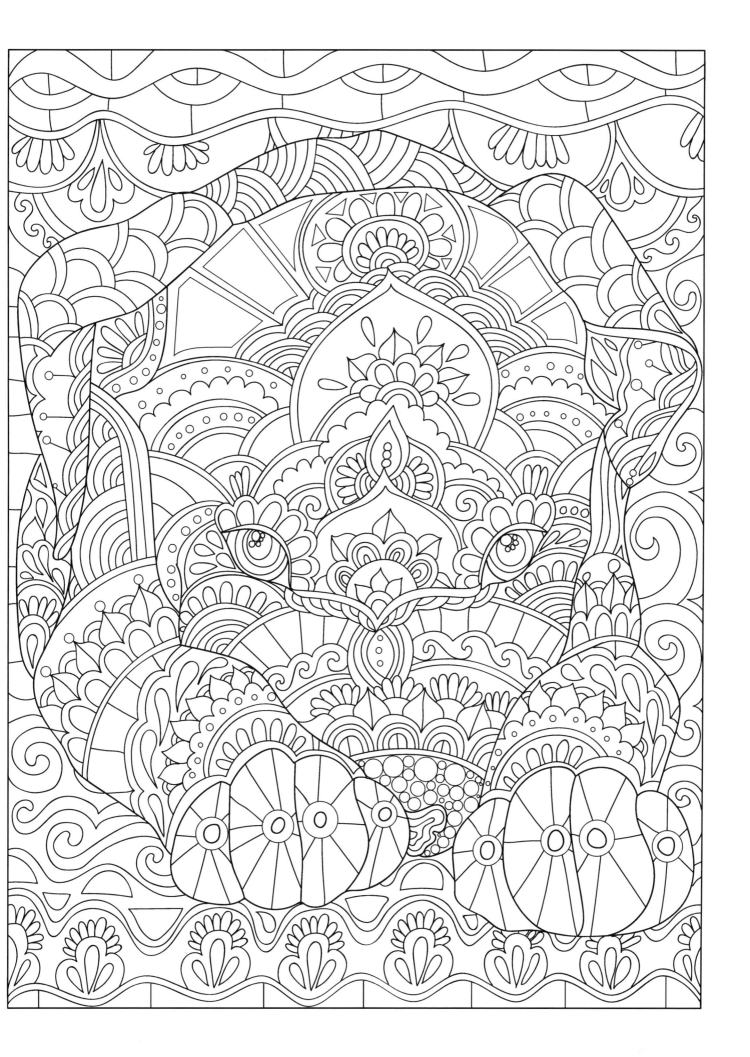

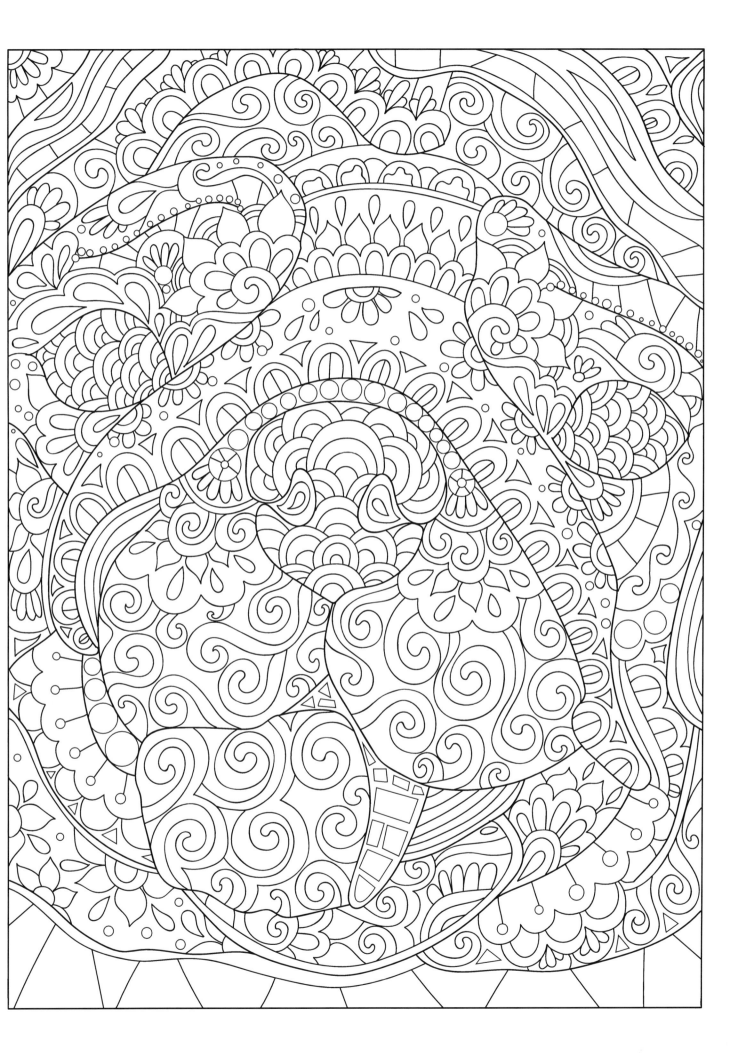

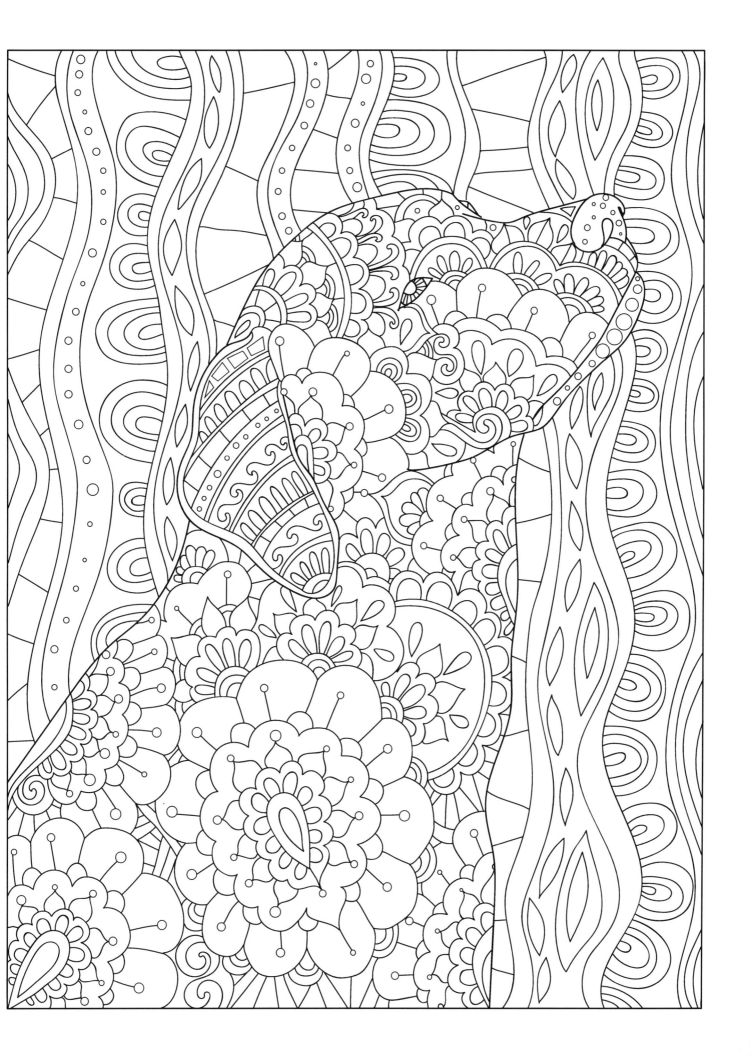

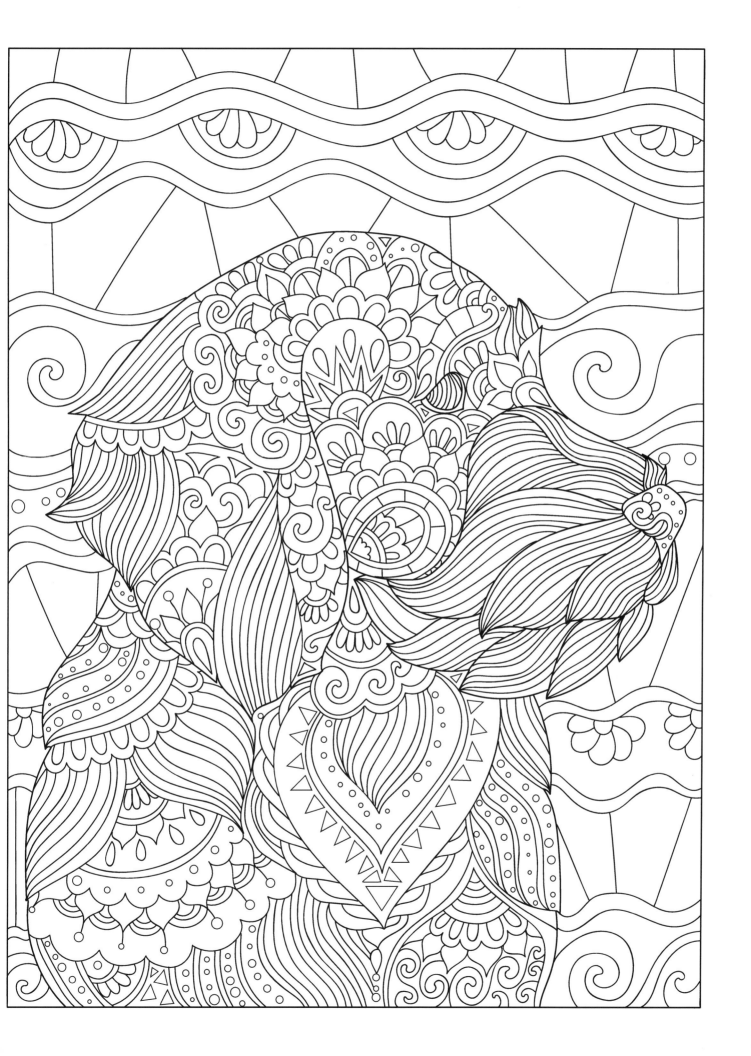

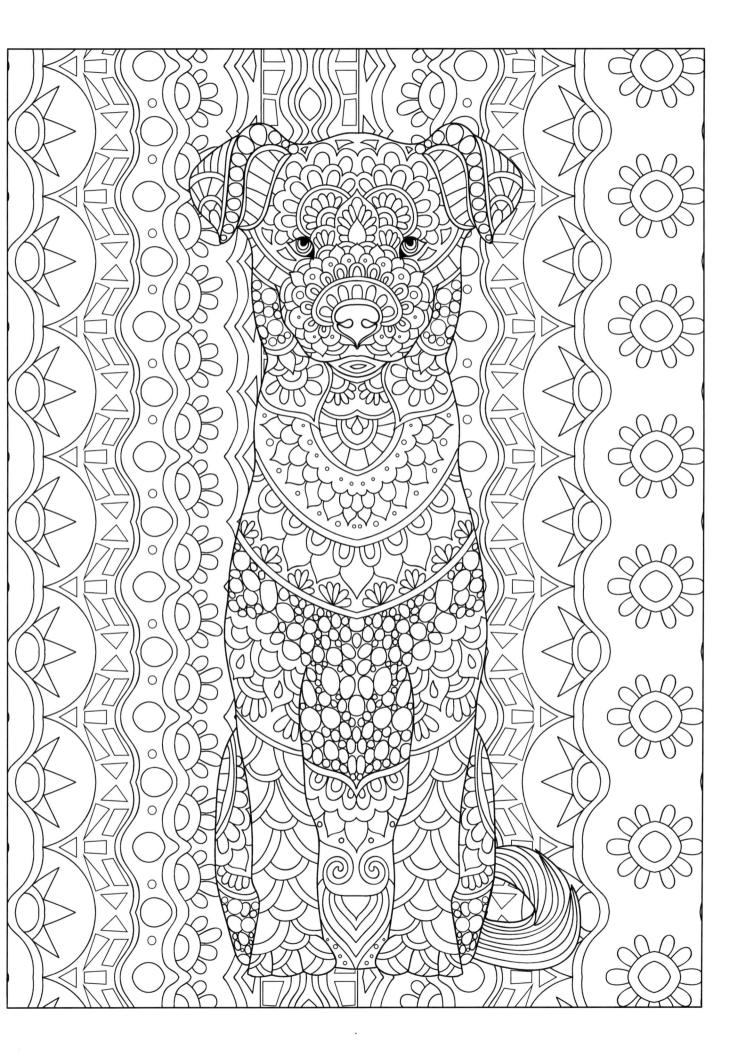

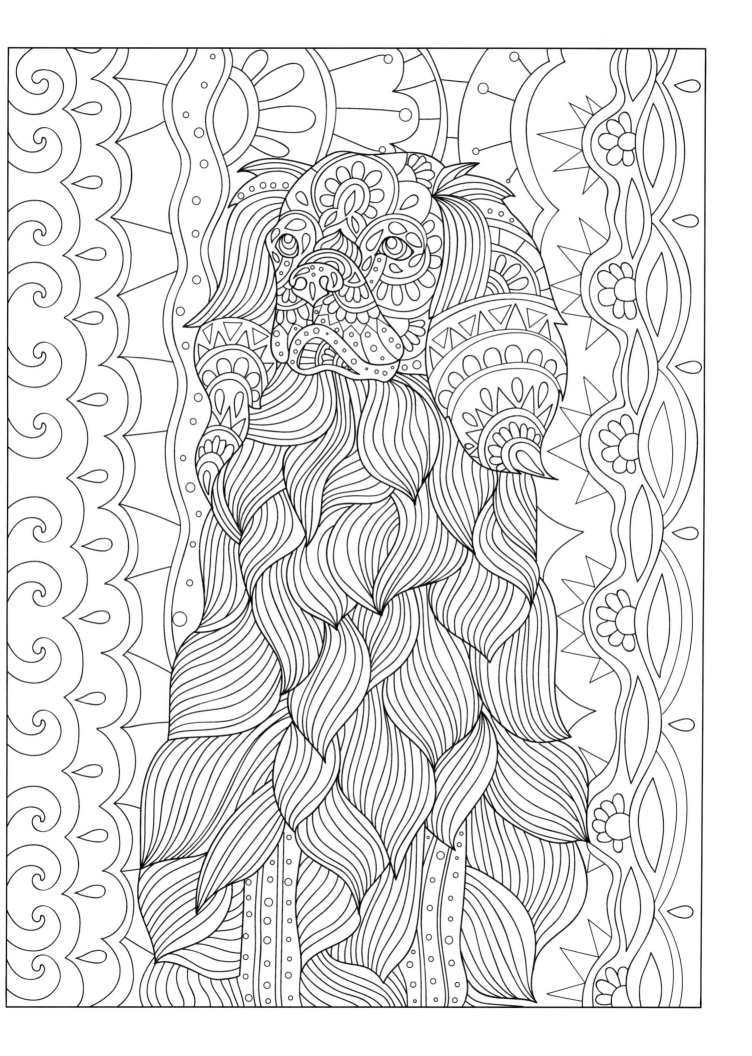

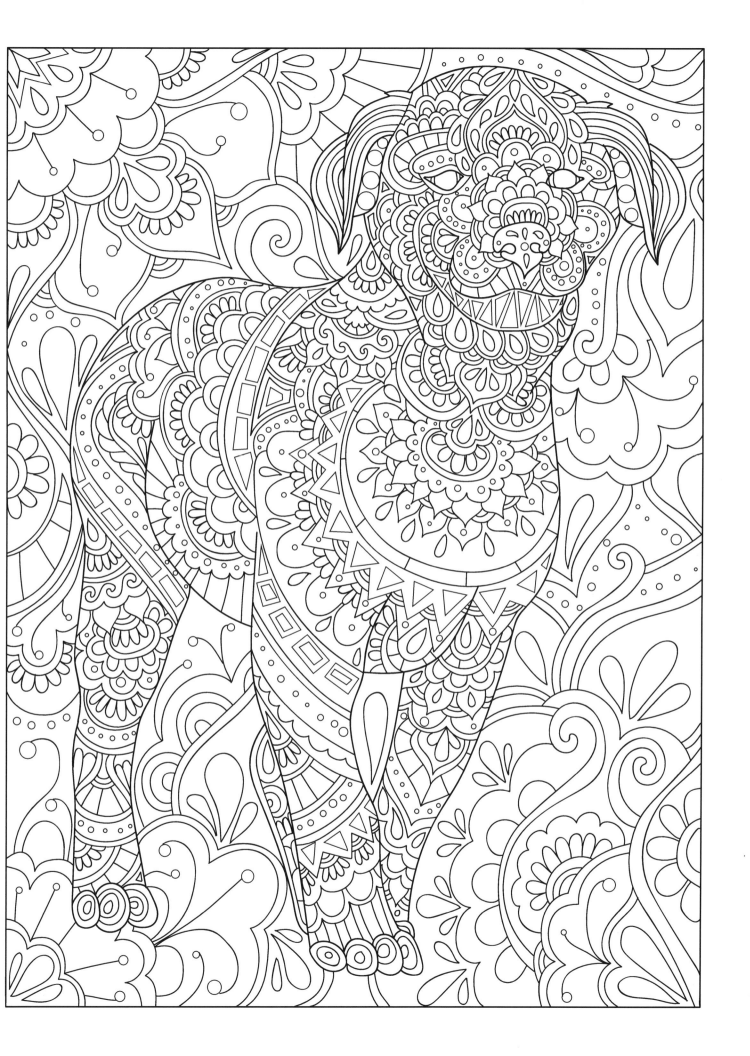

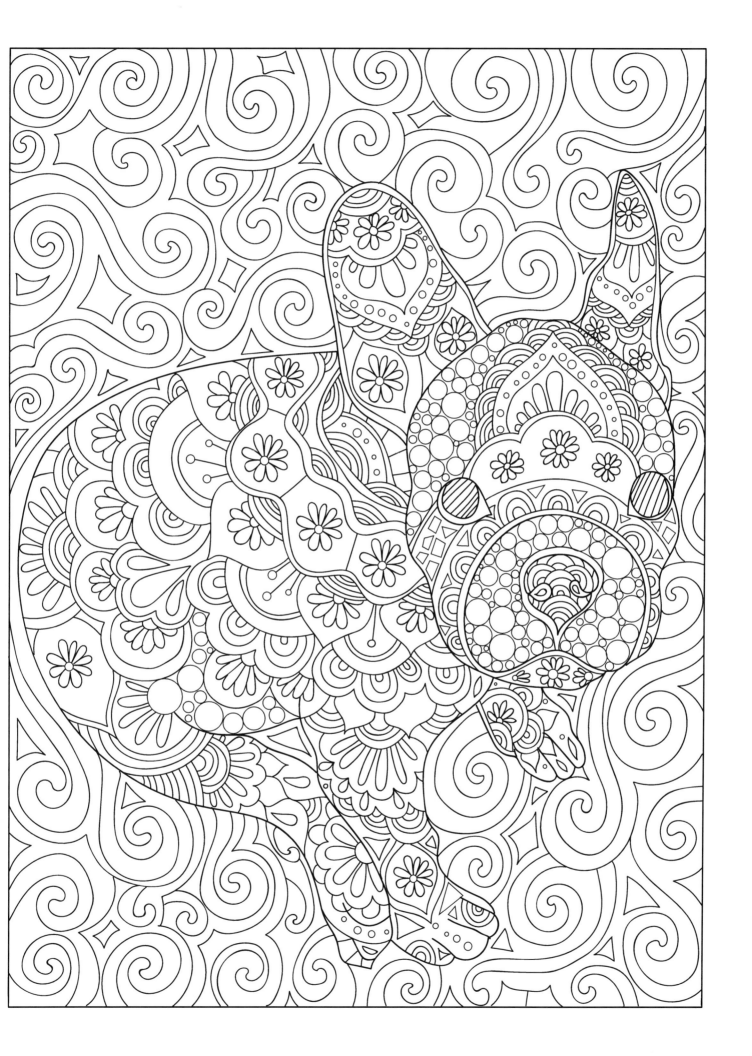

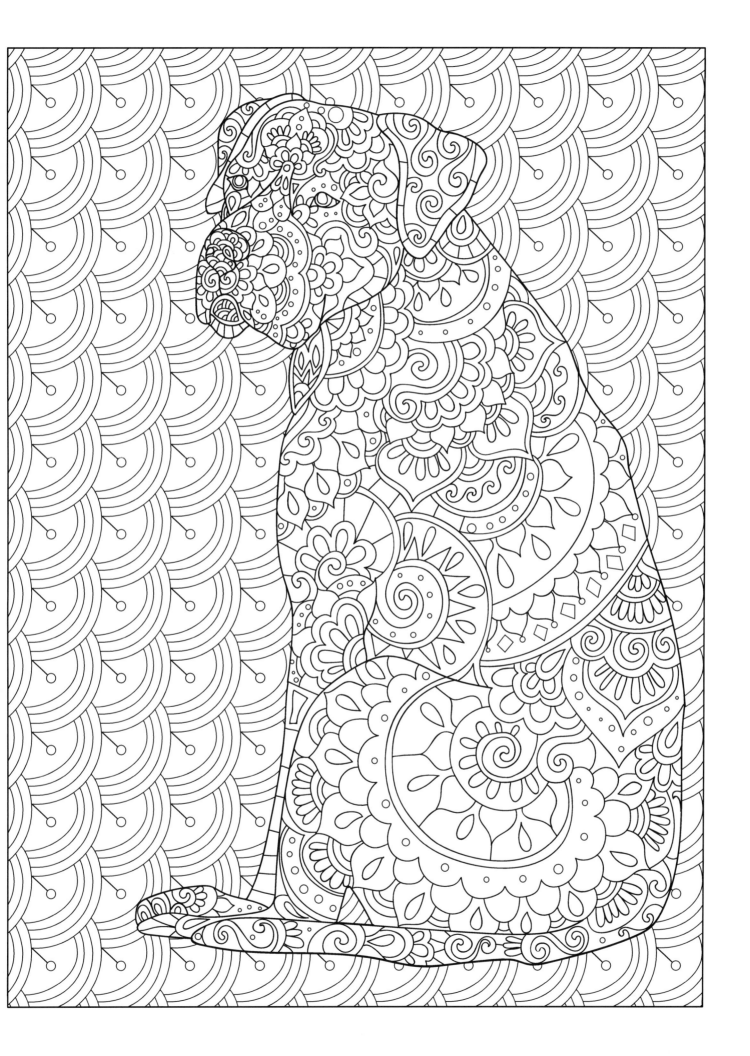

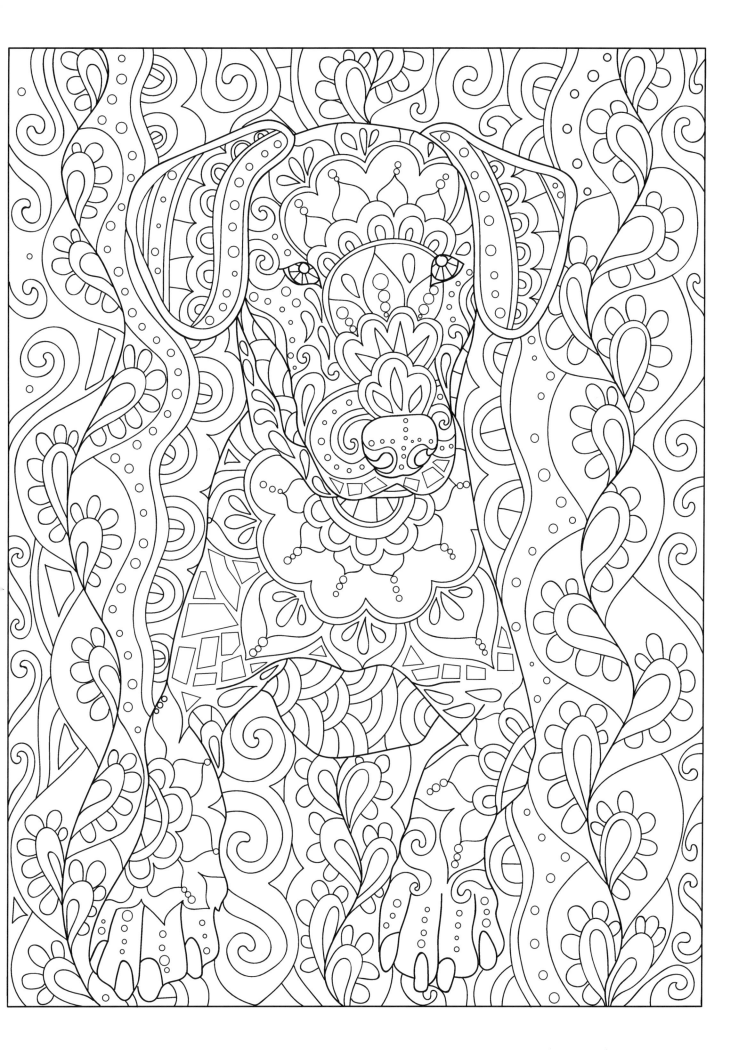

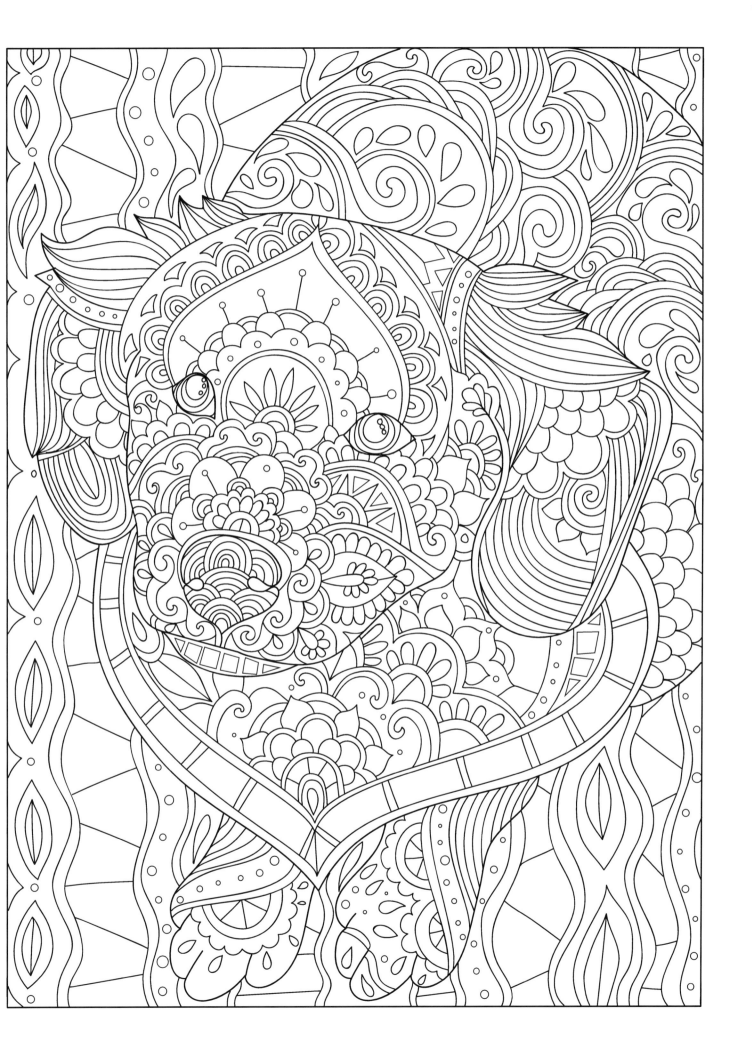

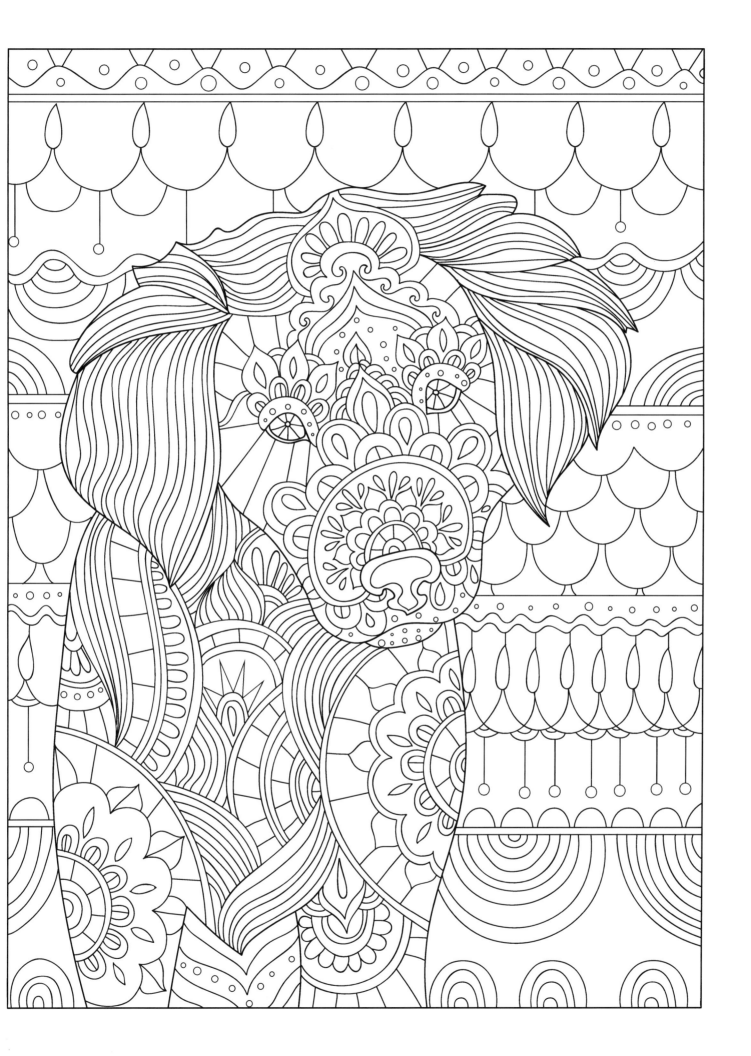

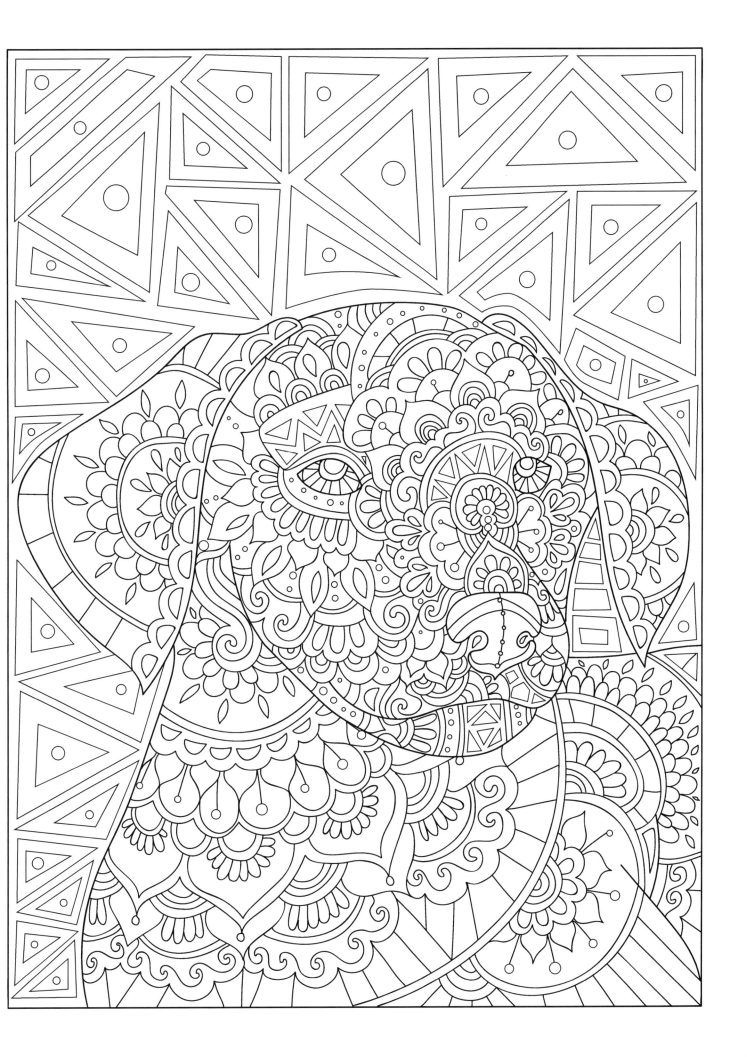

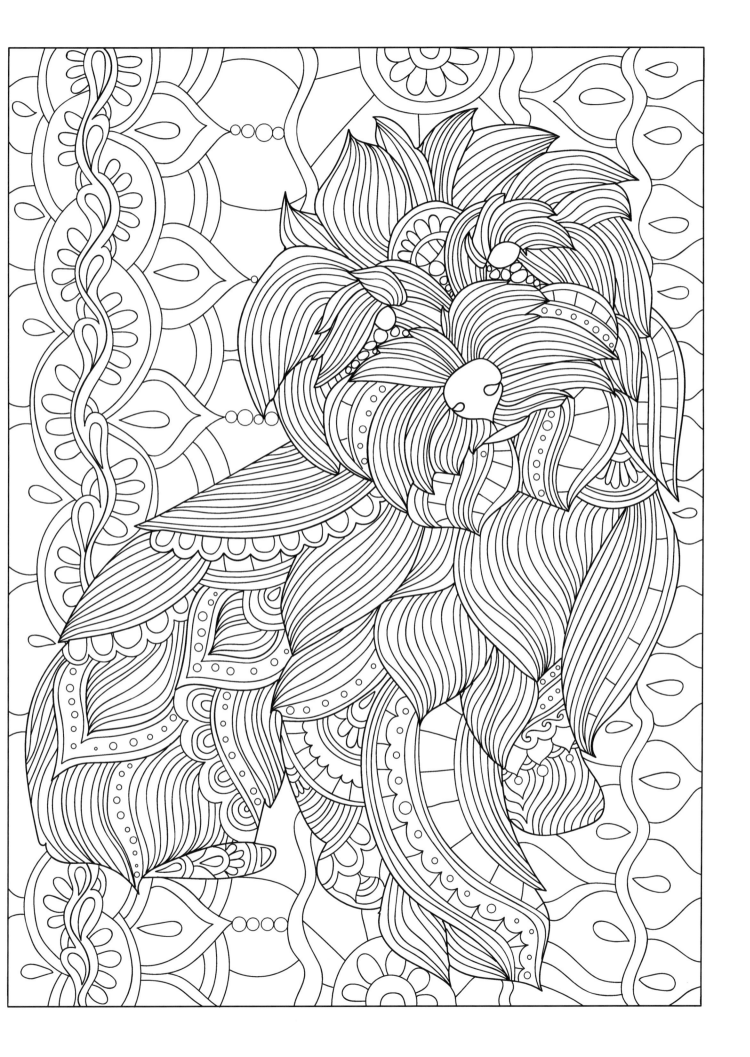

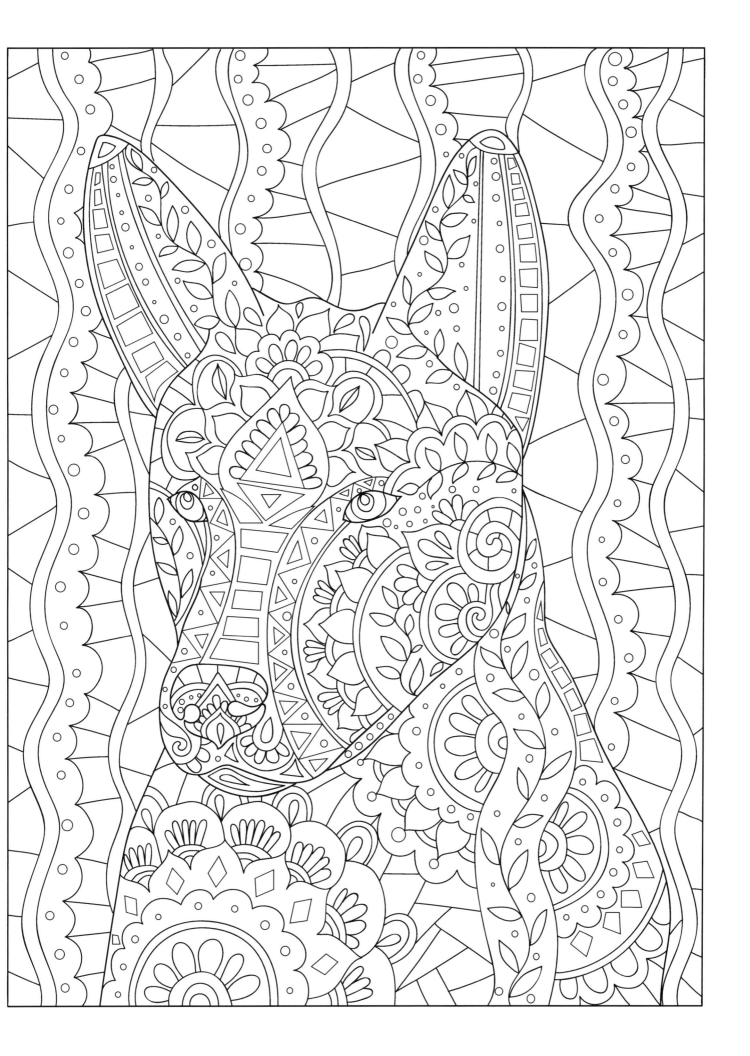

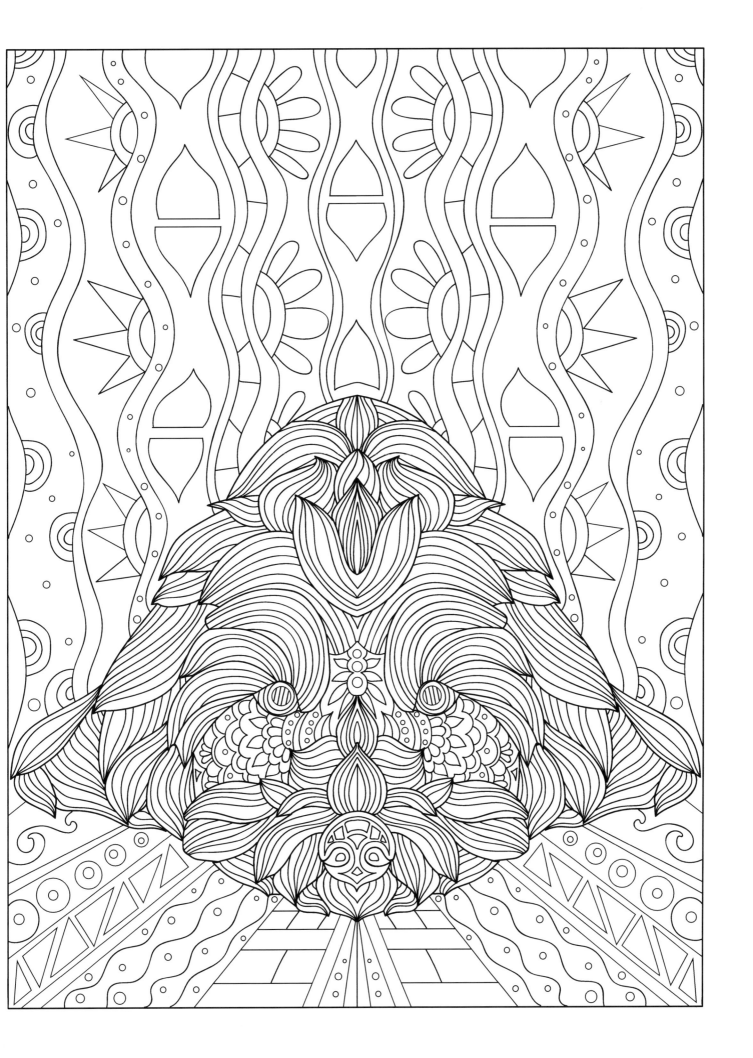

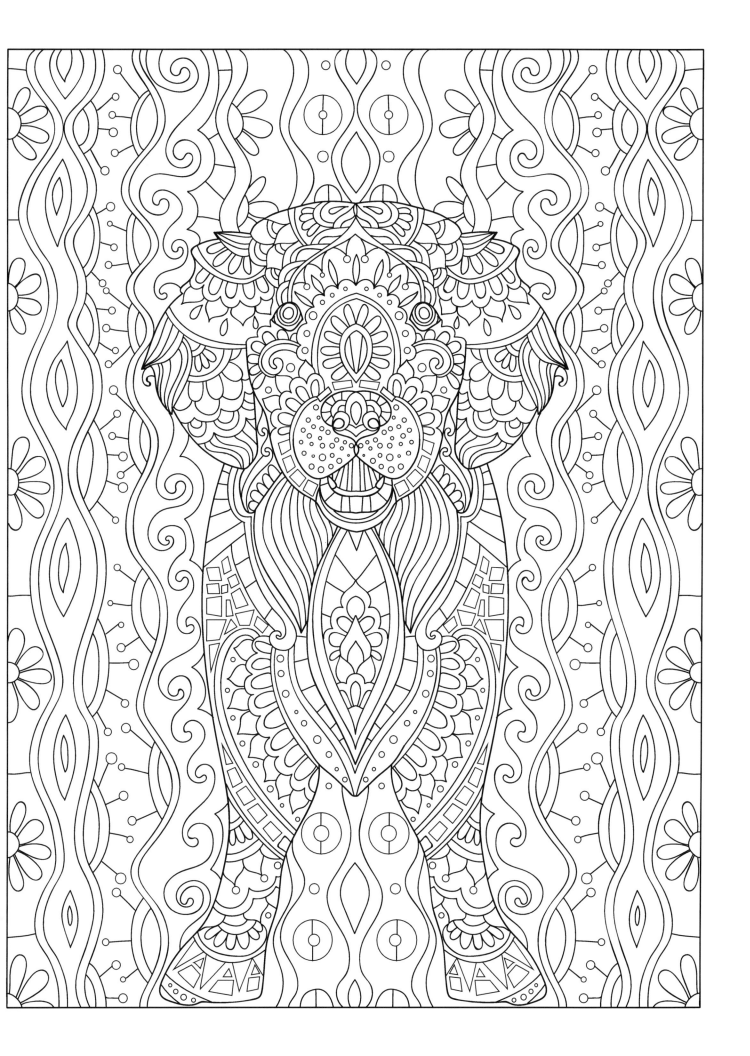

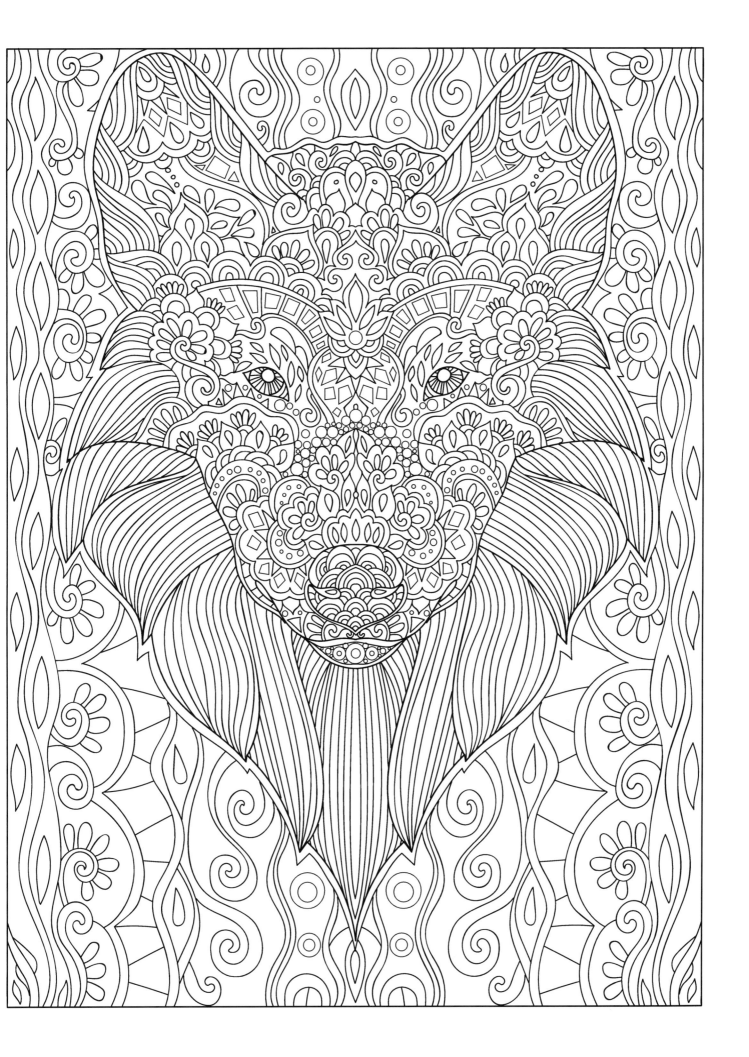

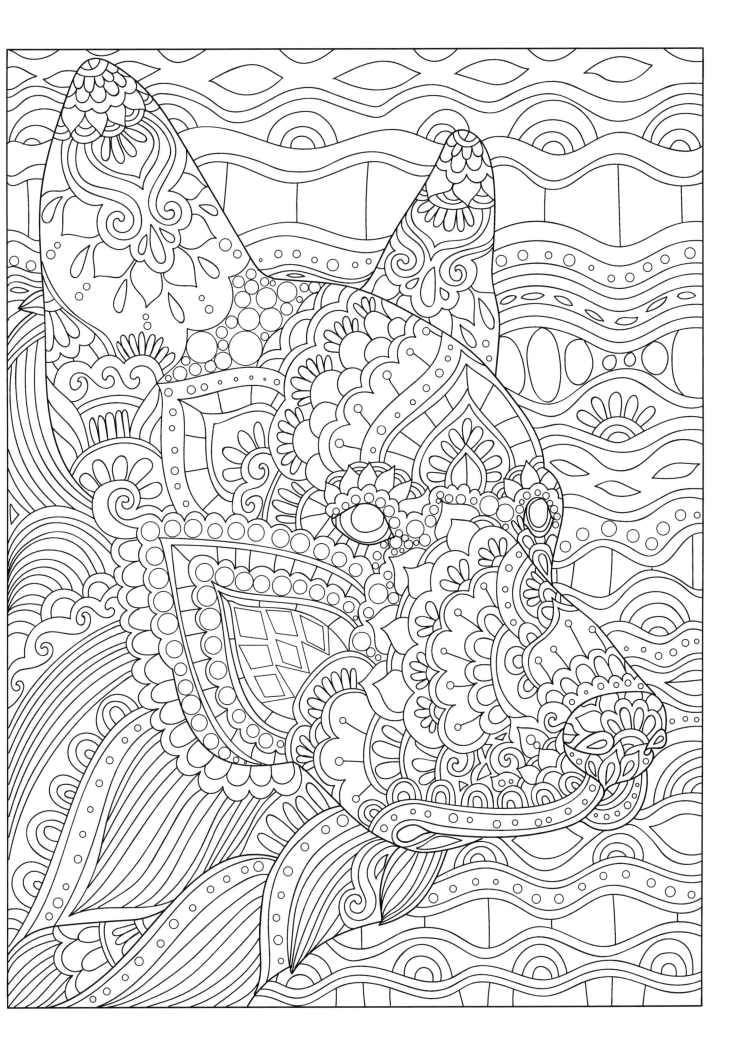

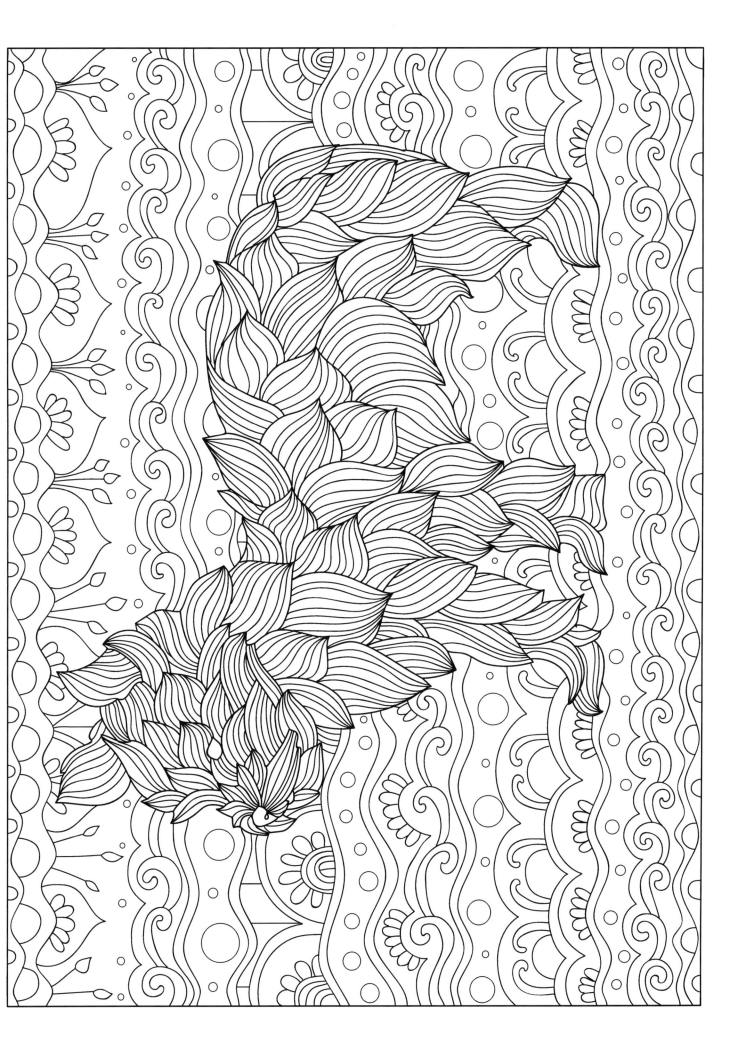

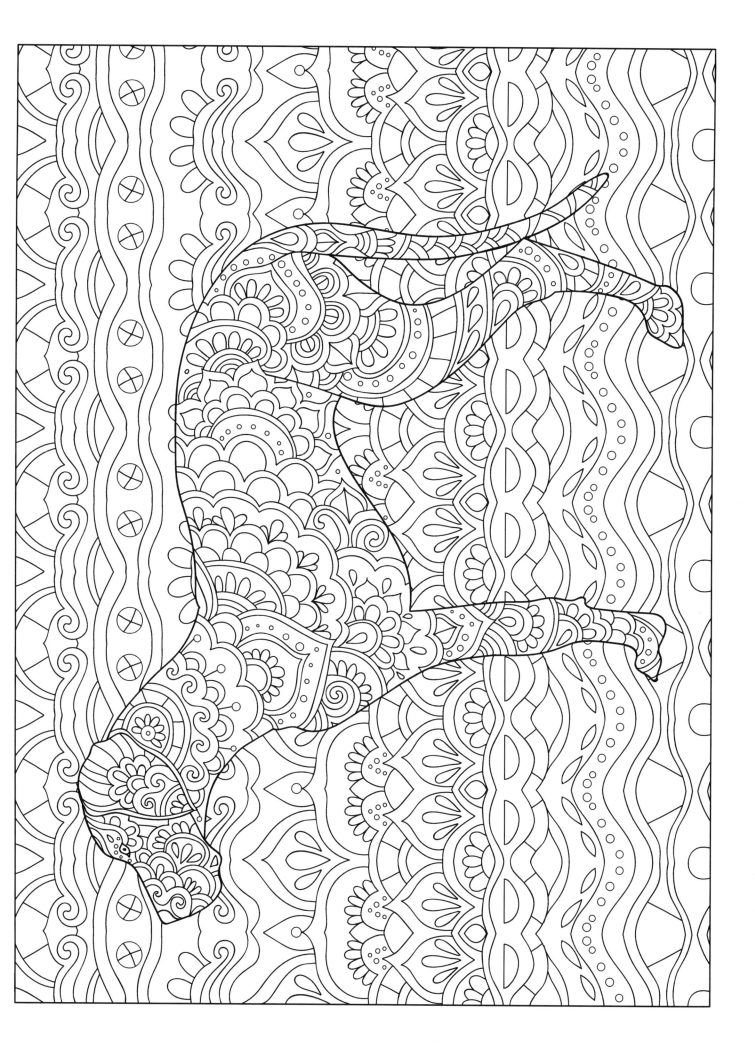

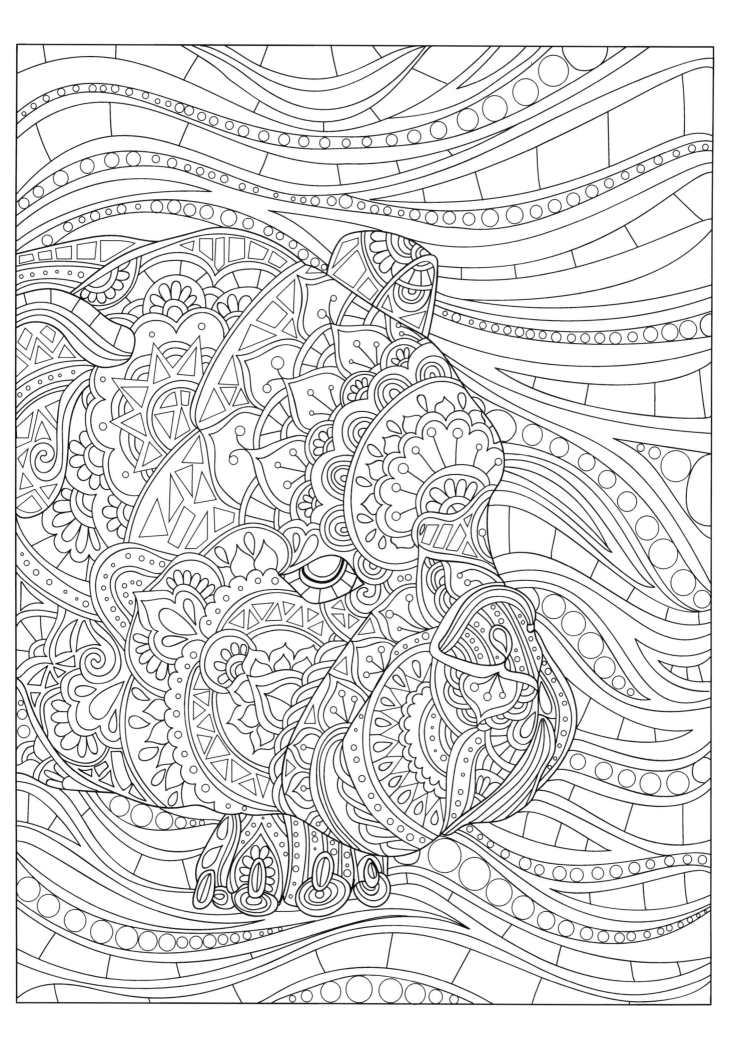

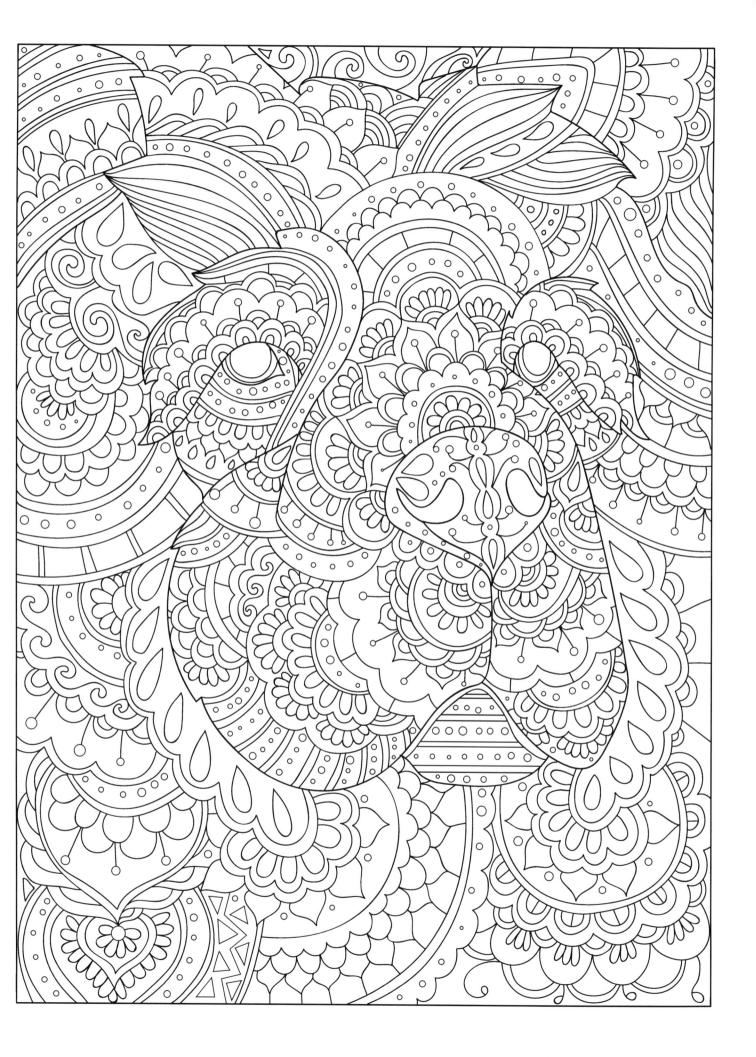

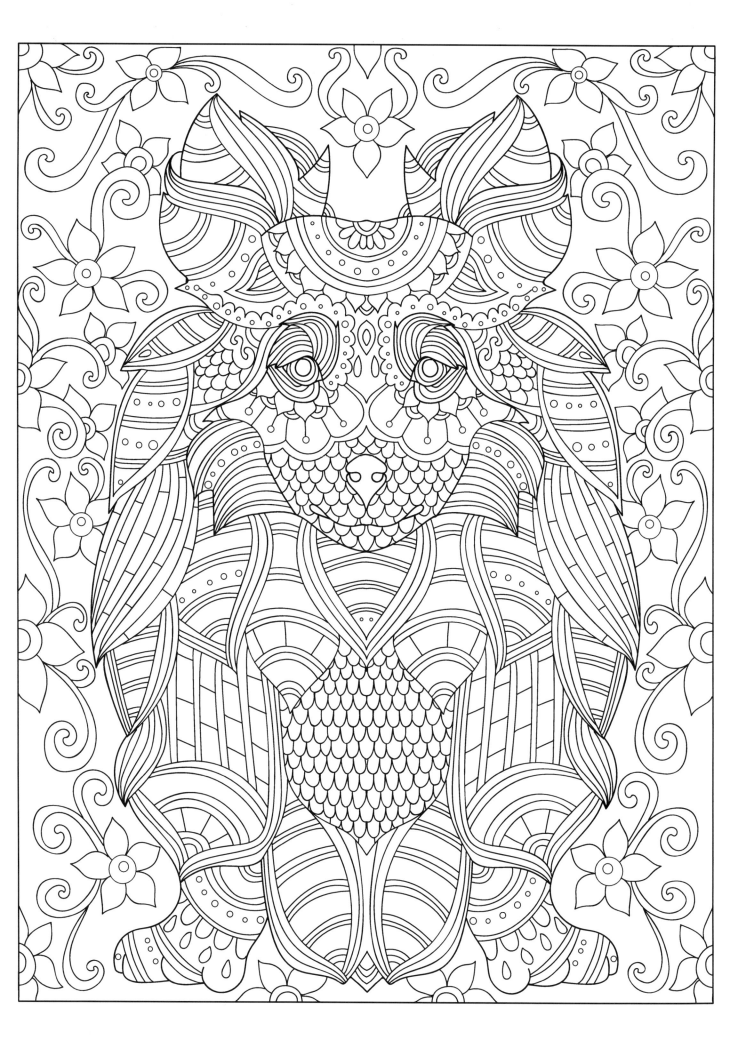

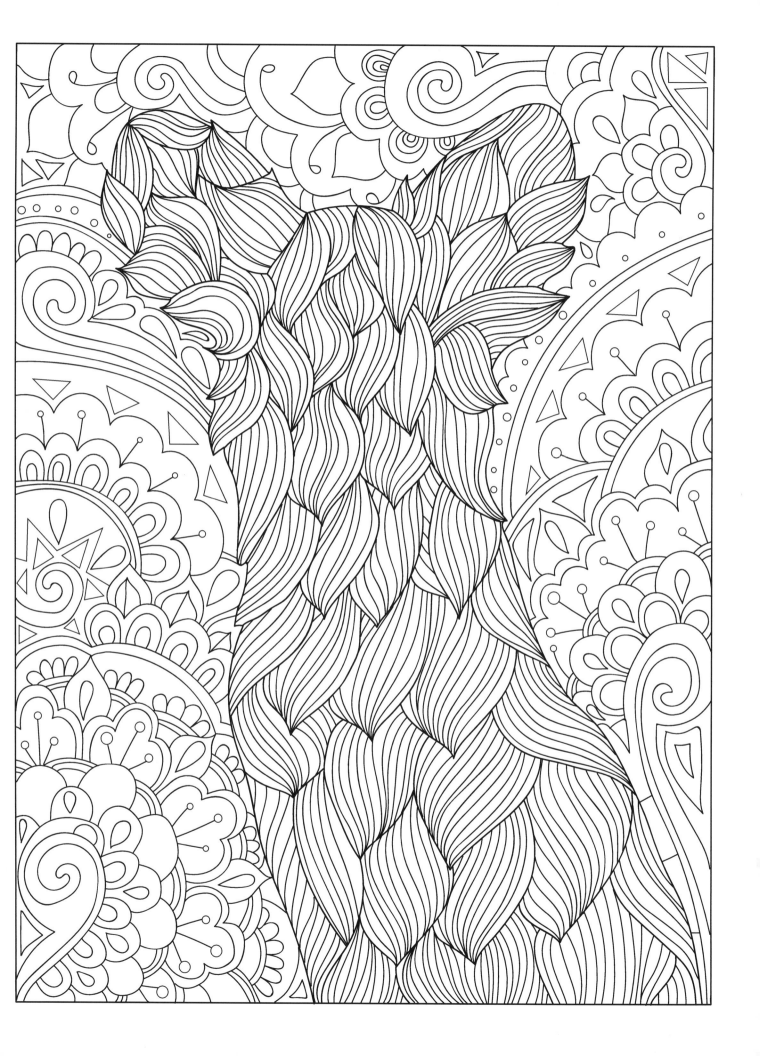

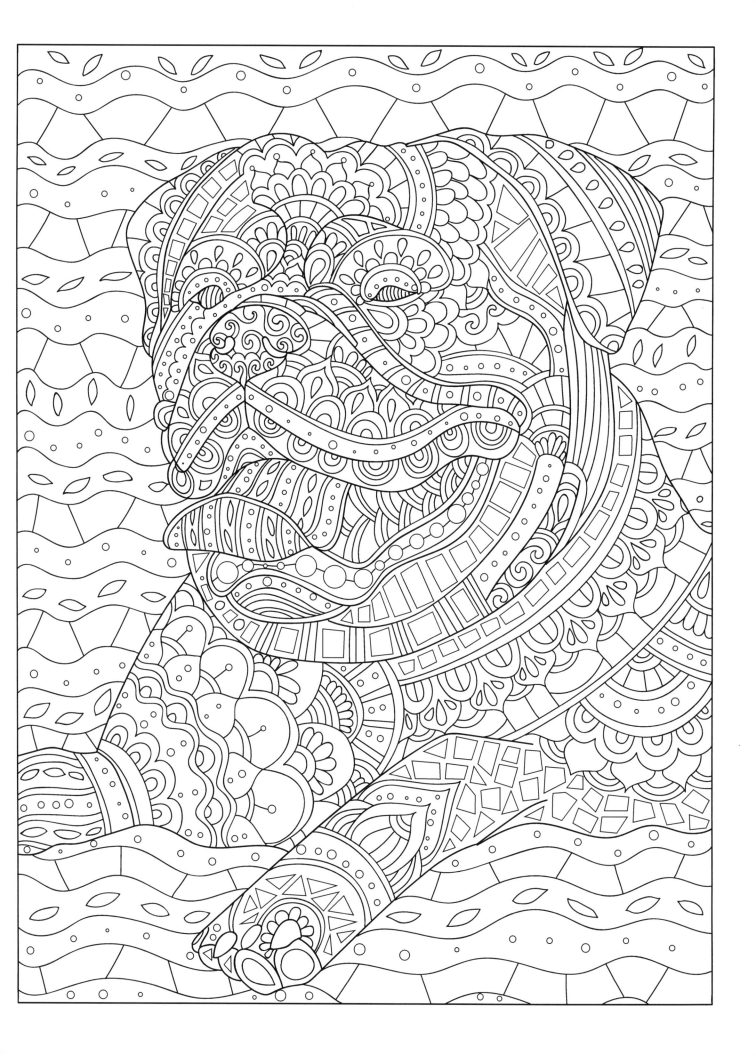

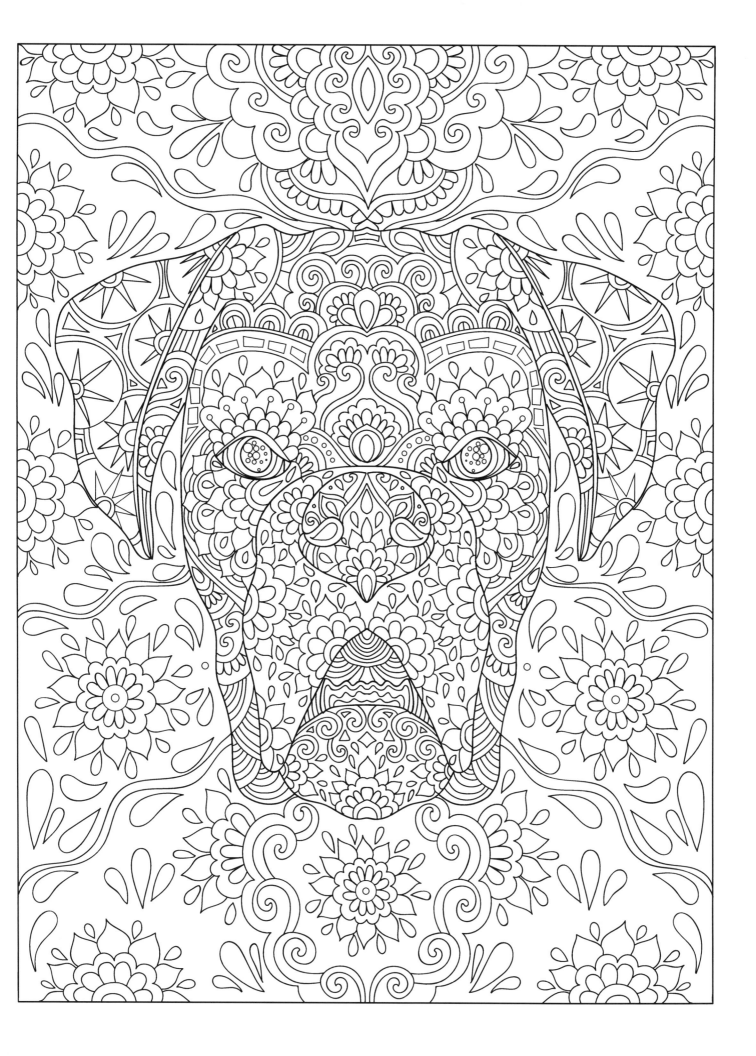

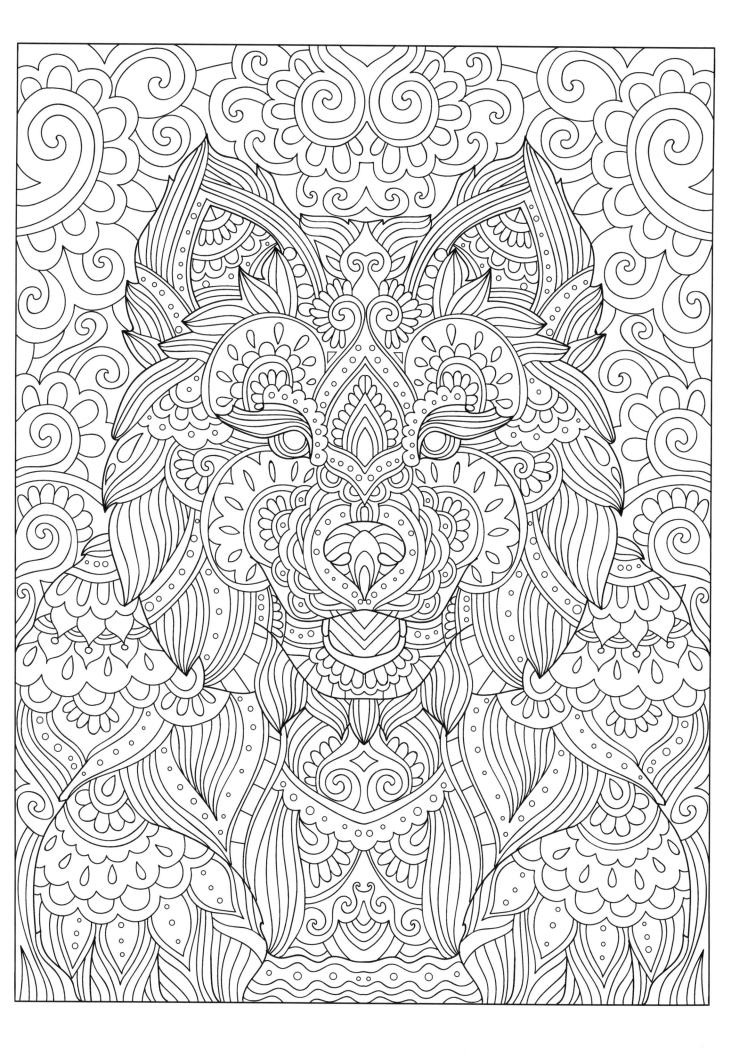

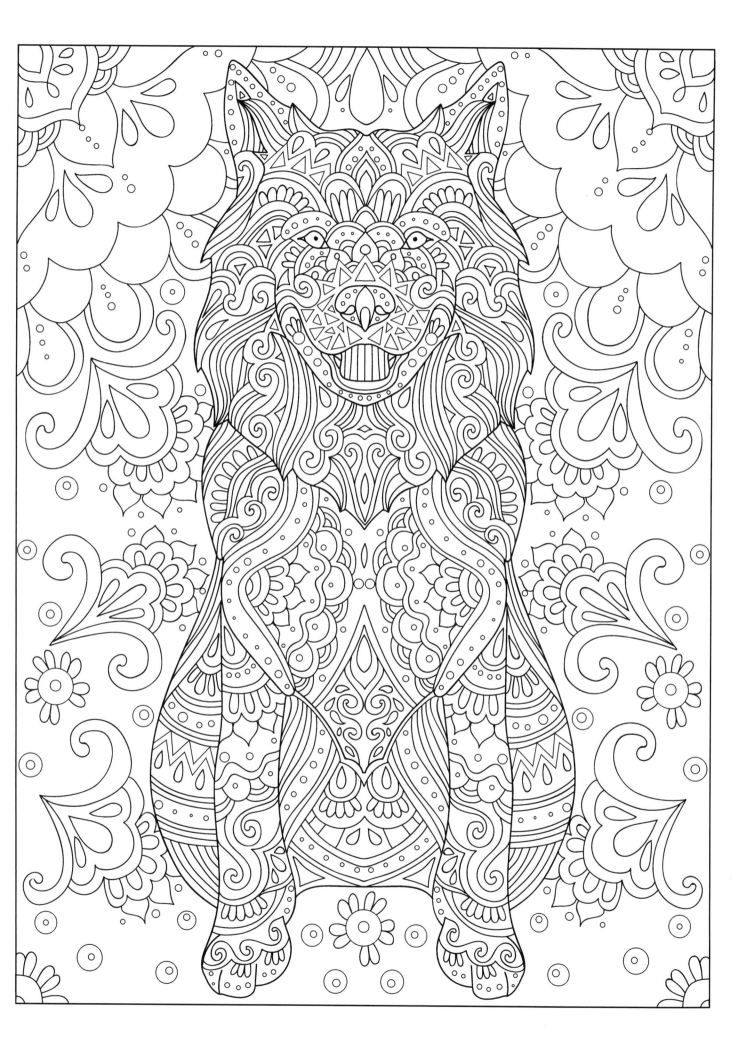

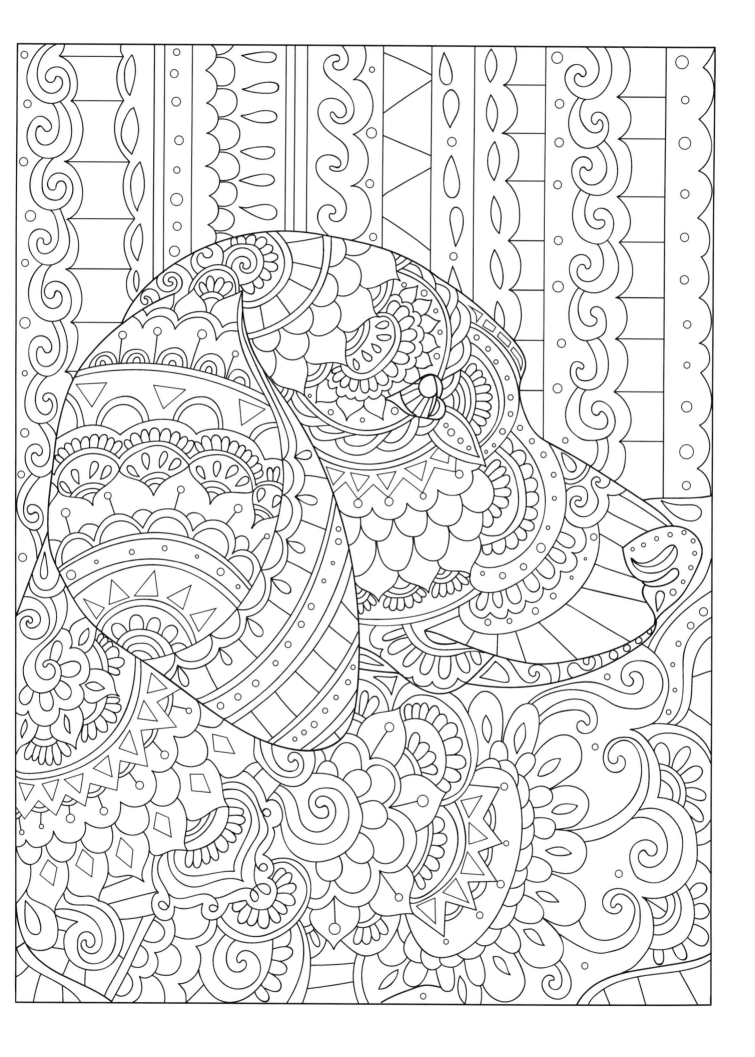

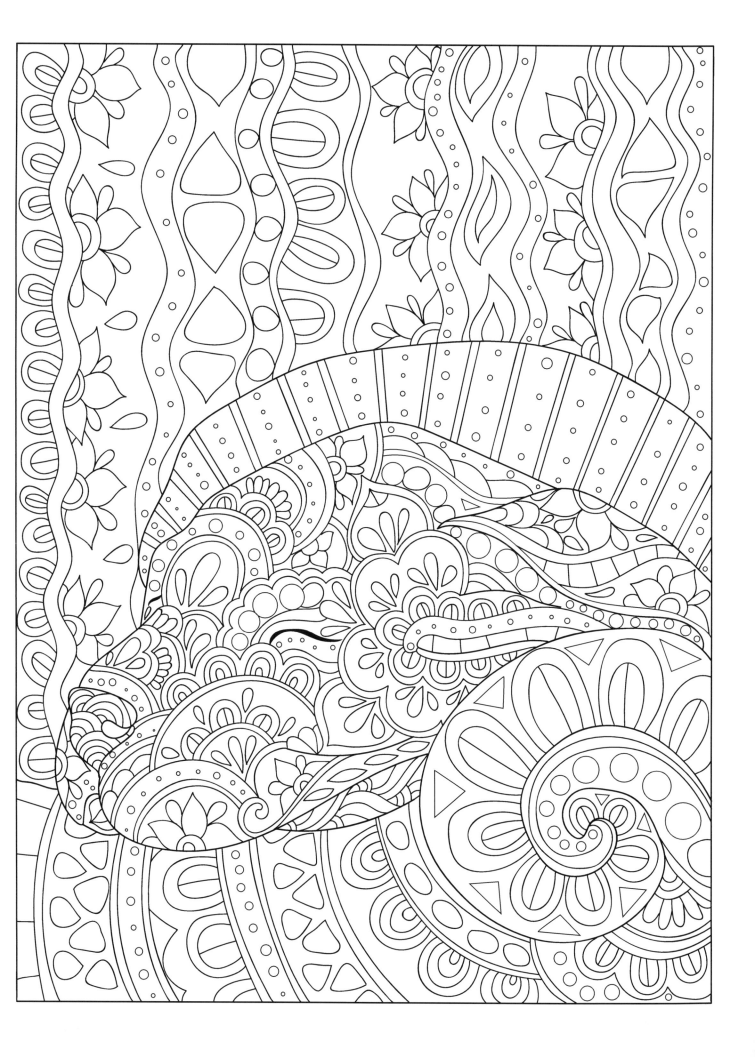

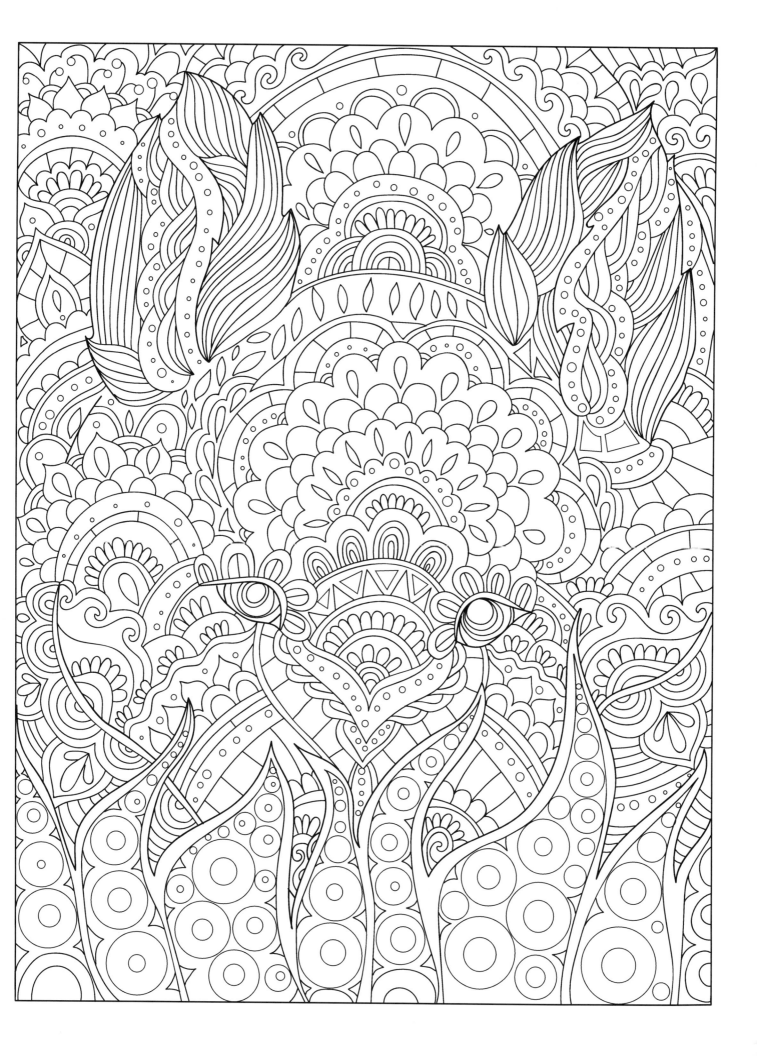

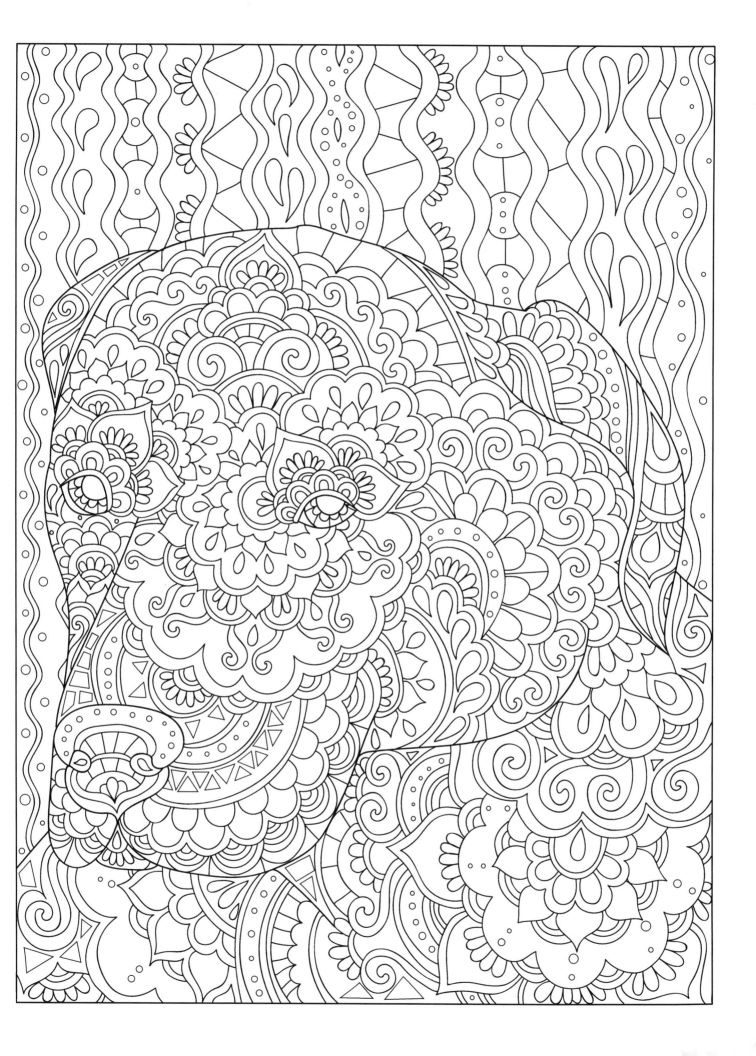

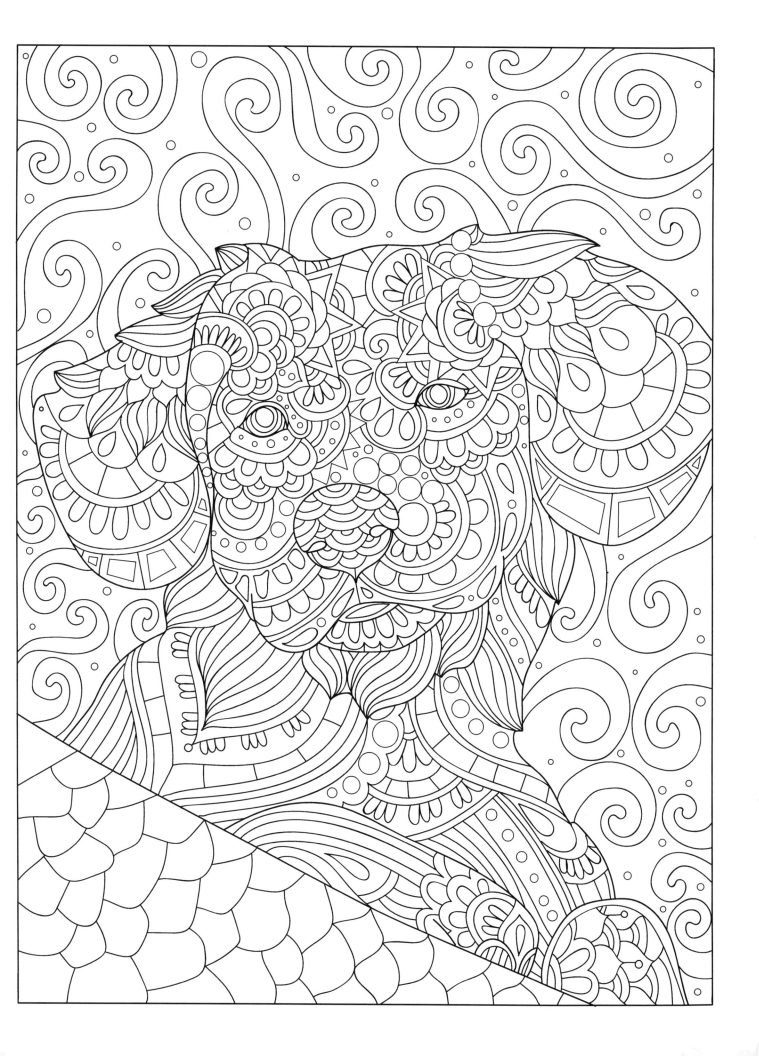

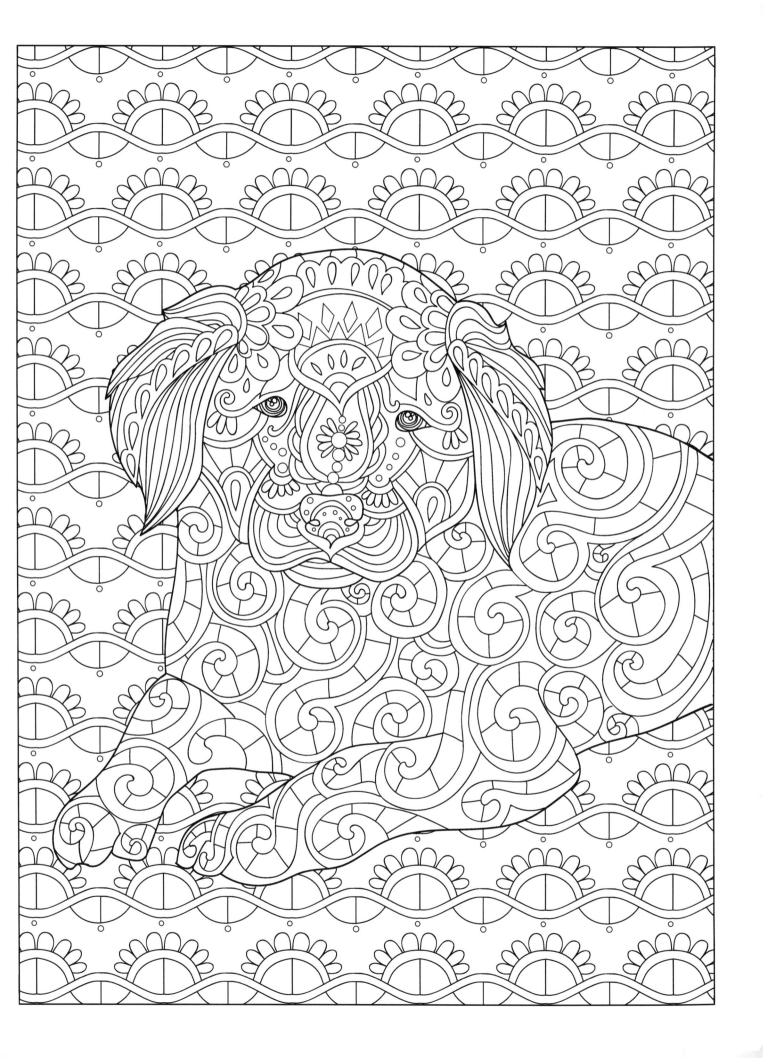

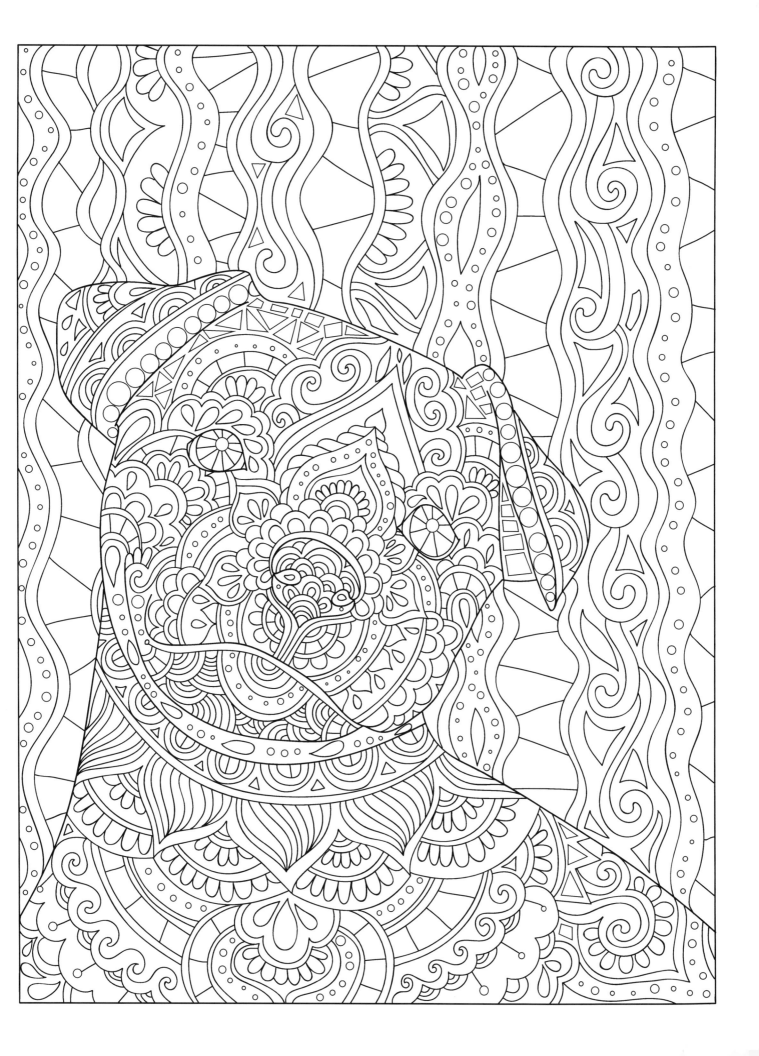

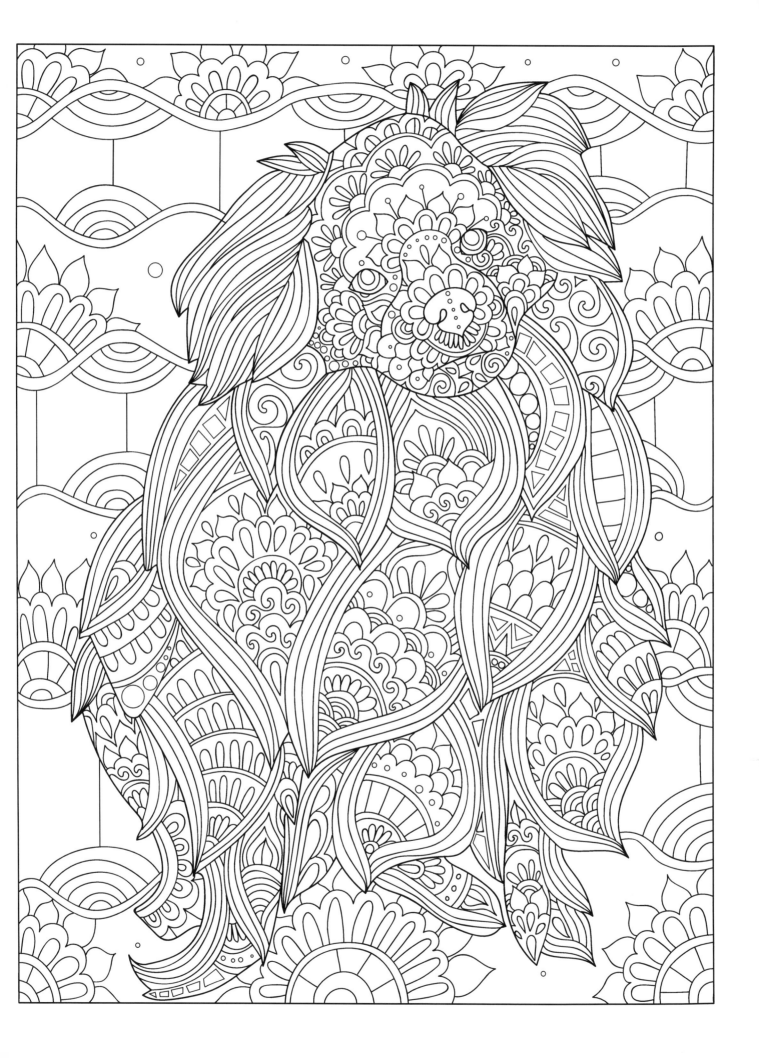

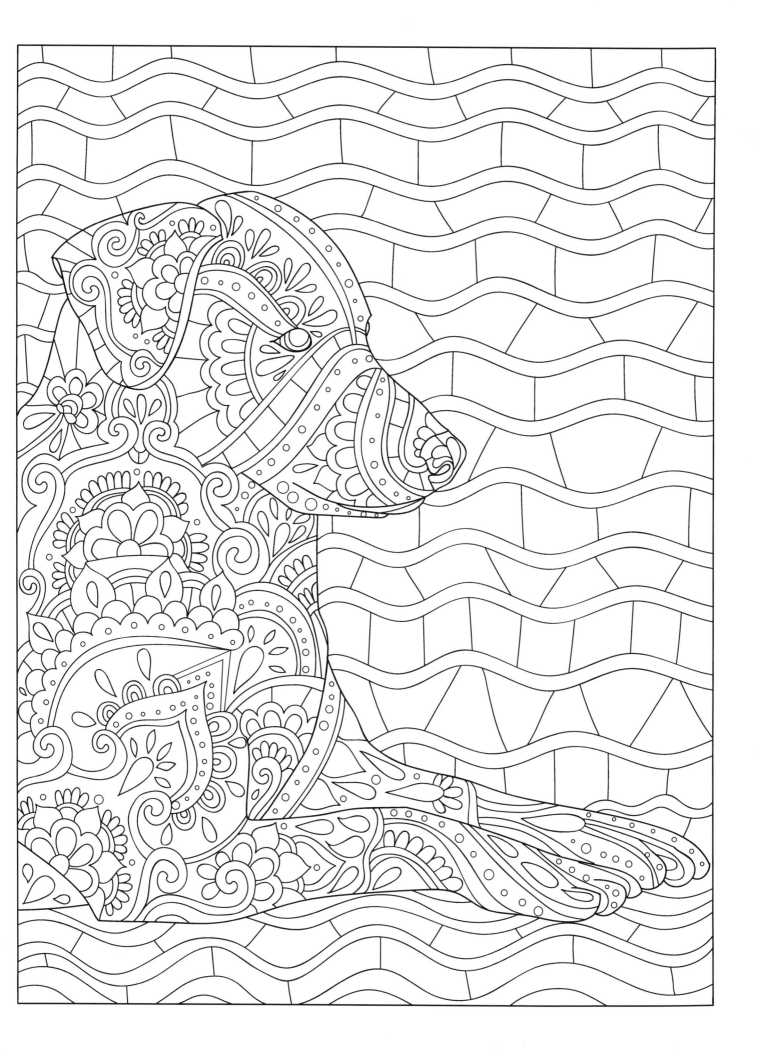

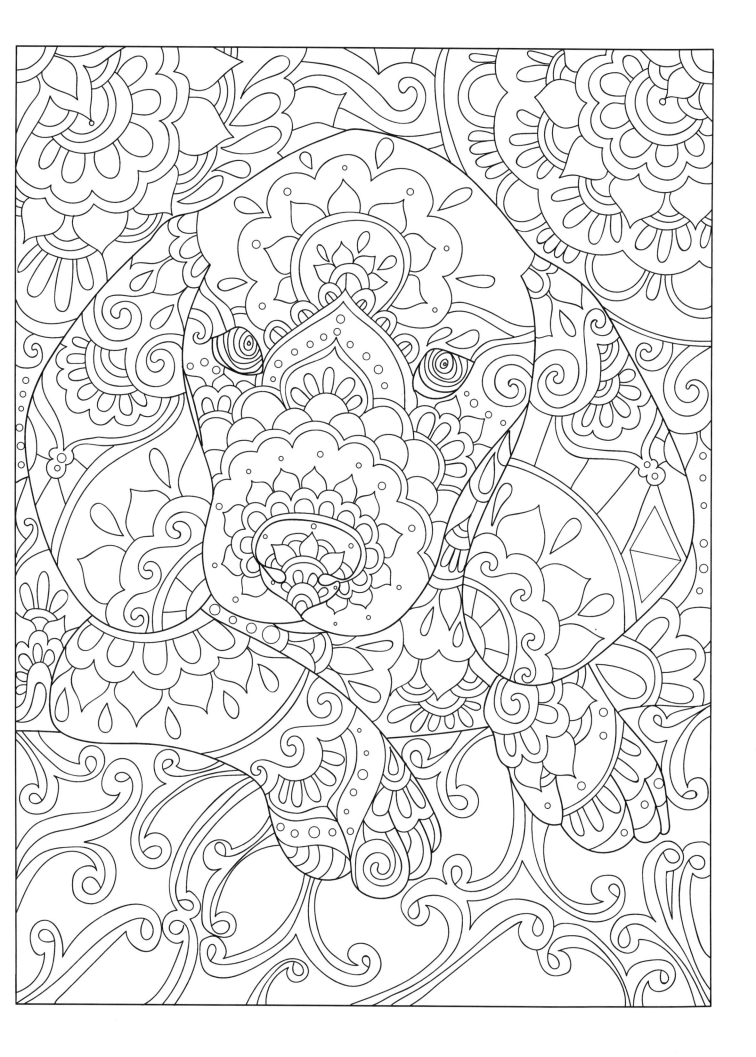

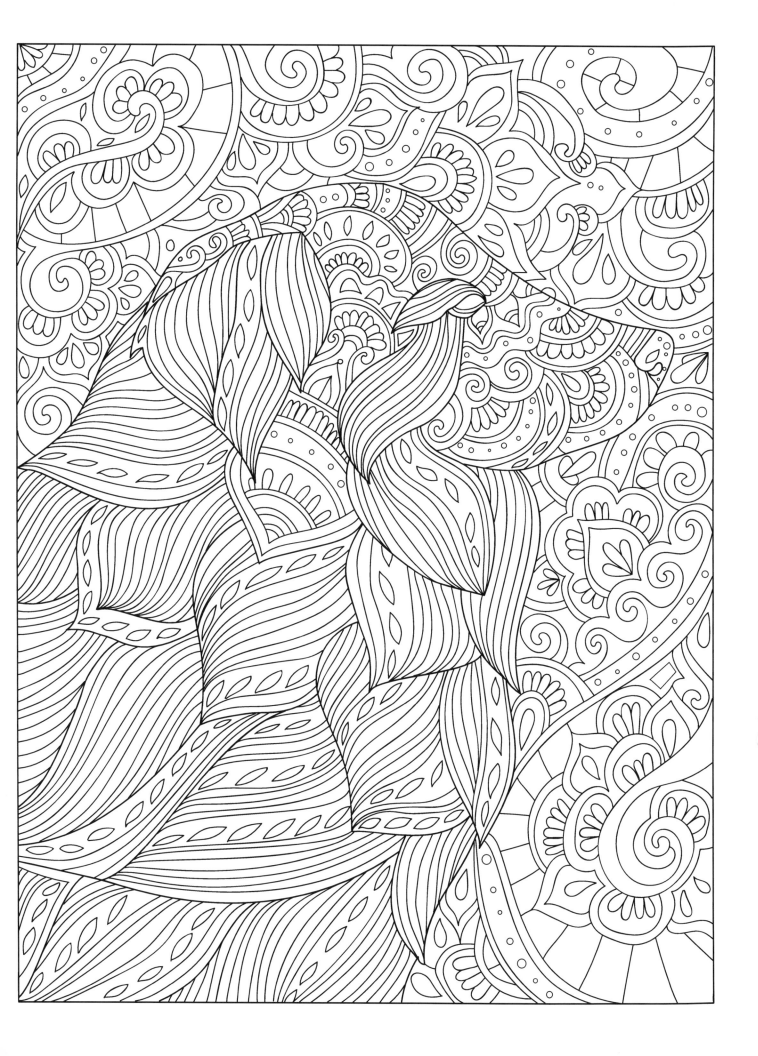

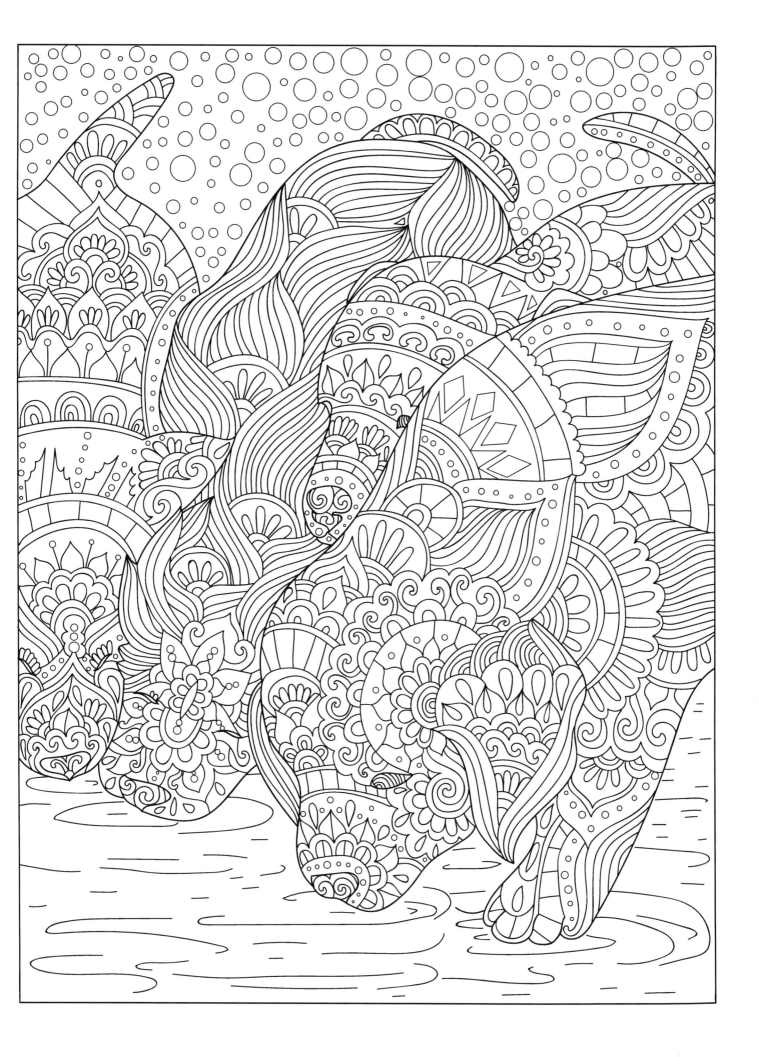

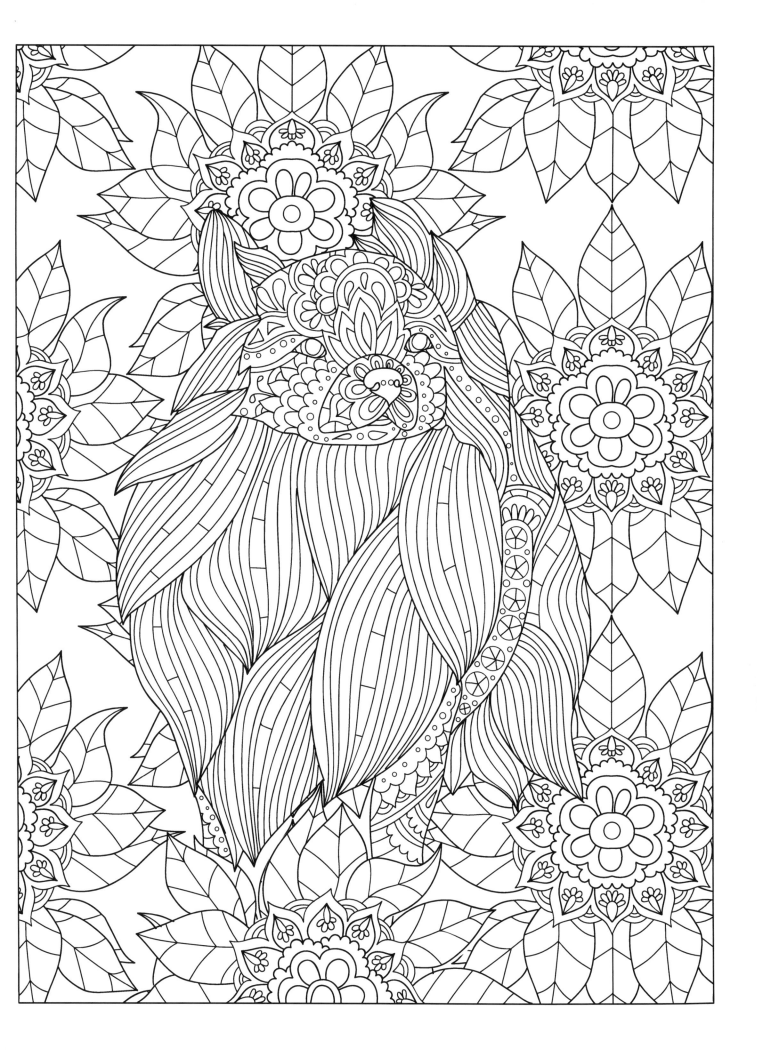

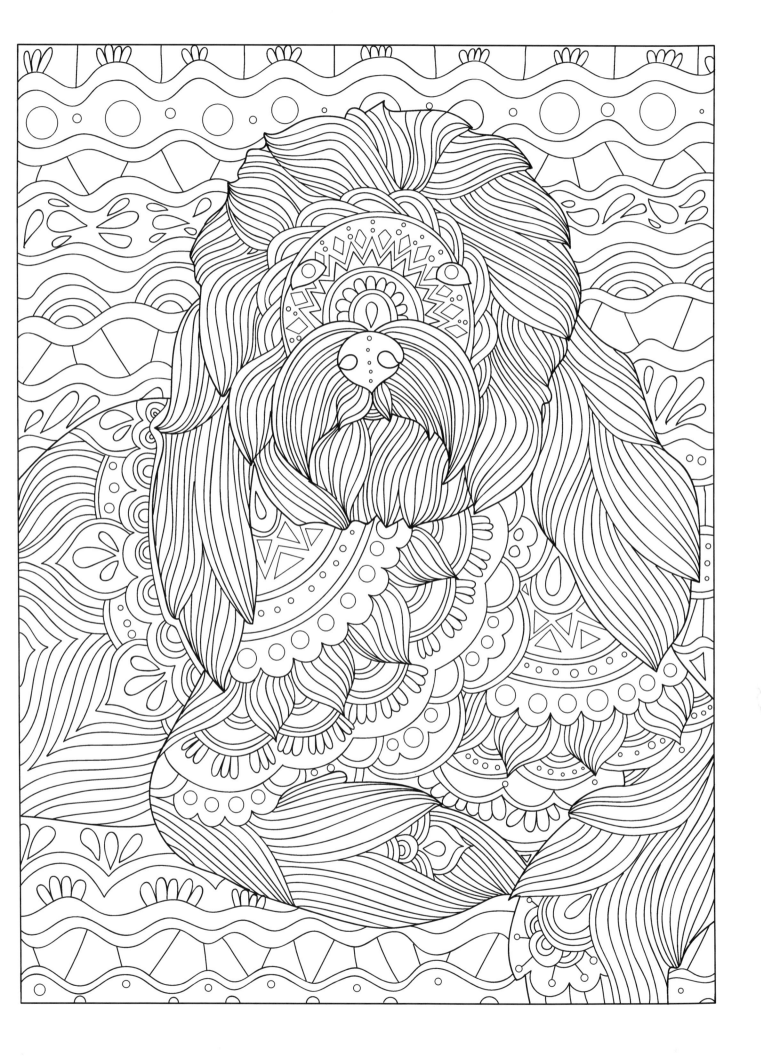

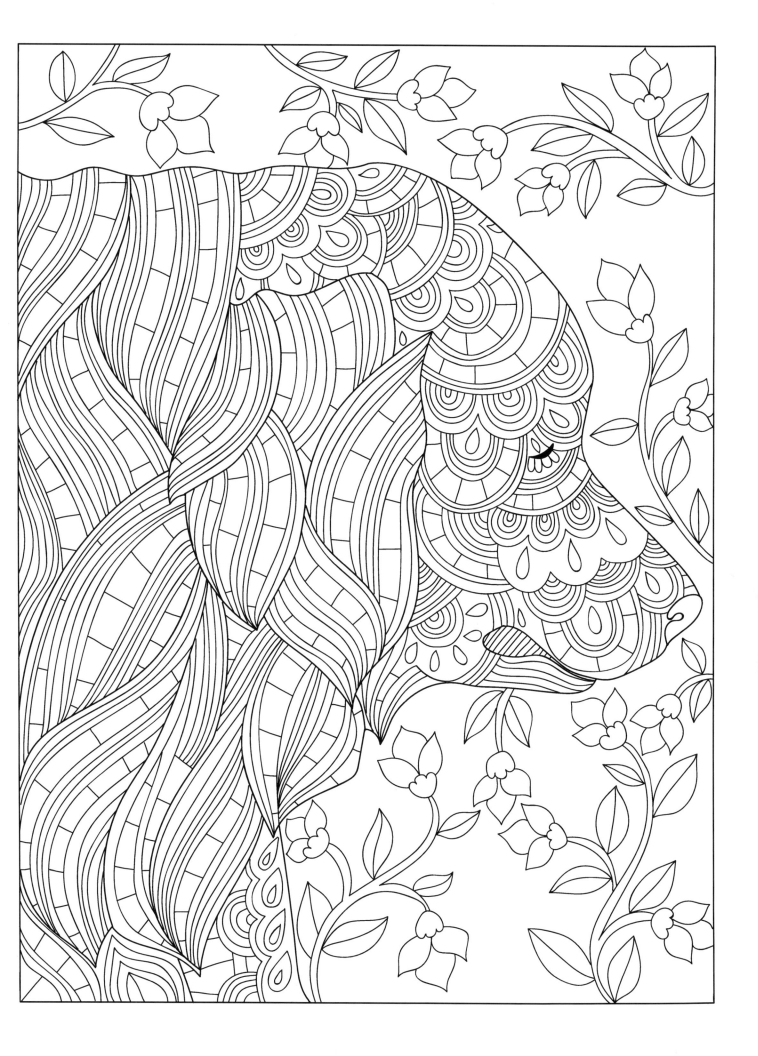

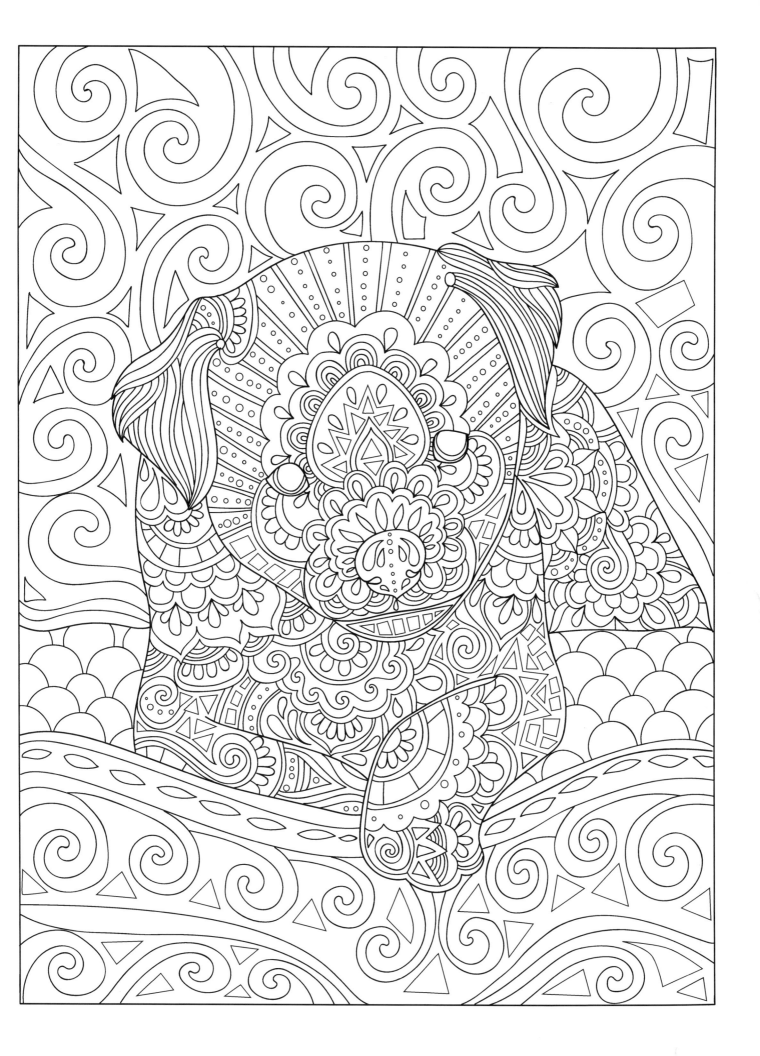

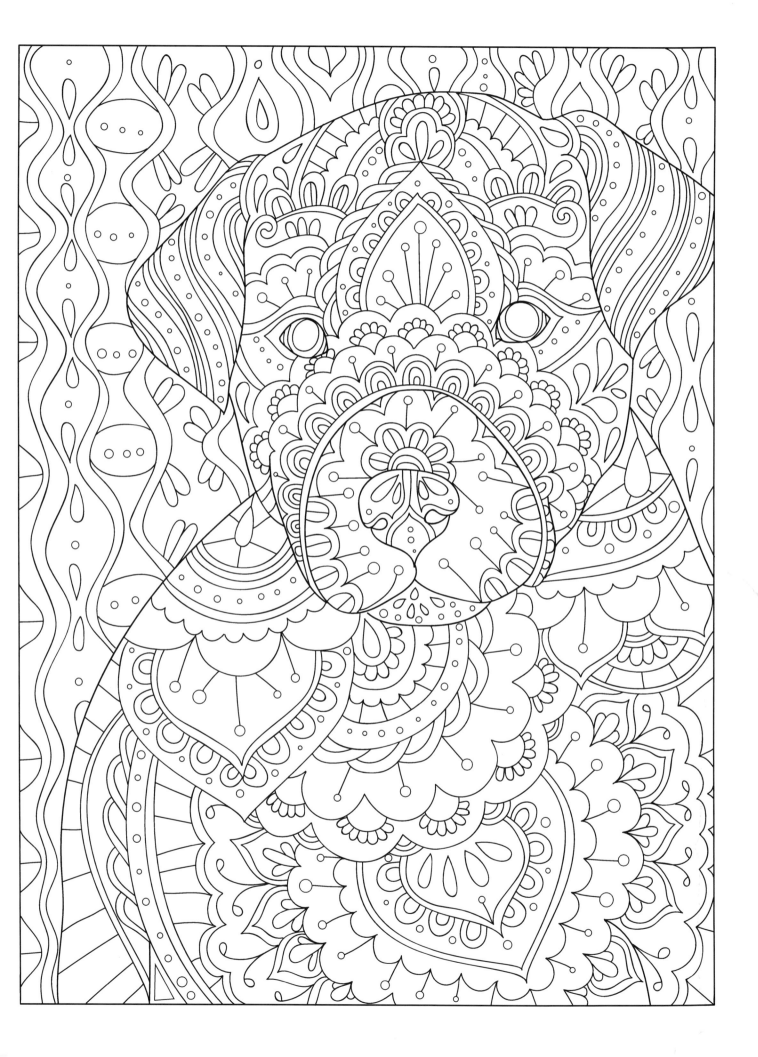

Made in the USA
Middletown, DE